# Where Have I Been?

# Where Have I Been?

# AN AUTOBIOGRAPHY

## WITH BILL DAVIDSON

*Crown Publishers, Inc.   New York*

# SID CAESAR

Copyright © 1982 by Sid Caesar Productions, Inc., and Bill Davidson.
All rights reserved. No part of this book may be reproduced or utilized in any form or by any means, electronic or mechanical, including photocopying, recording, or by any information storage and retrieval system, without permission in writing from the publisher.
Published by Crown Publishers, Inc., One Park Avenue, New York,
New York 10016 and published simultaneously in Canada
by General Publishing Company Limited
Manufactured in the United States of America
Library of Congress Cataloging in Publication Data
Caesar, Sid, 1922—
Where have I been?
1. Caesar, Sid, 1922–   .   2. Entertainers—
United States—Biography. I. Davidson, Bill,
1918–   .   II. Title.
PN2287.C22A38 1982       791.45′028′0924 [B]       82-9965
ISBN: 0-517-547945                                 AACR2
Designed by Camilla Filancia
10 9 8 7 6 5 4 3 2 1
First Edition

# Contents

# Contents

*Photographs appear following pages 88 and 184.*

To Florence, Shelly, Rick, Karen, and Maranee—
who shared it all with me.          SID CAESAR


As always, to Muriel.          BILL DAVIDSON


# Preface

I am an entertainer; so in much of this book, I entertain.

My main purpose in telling my story, however, is to give hope to all those people with such vast personal problems that living has become suffering—as it did for me.

I want them to know they are not alone.

God knows, if *I* could learn to conquer my overwhelming fears, addictions, and self-doubts, certainly others can learn to banish their own demons.

And reestablish belief in themselves.          SID CAESAR

# Prologue

## *The Glory Years*

Carl Reiner, the airport reporter, is interviewing Sid Caesar, as Professor Von Houdinoff, an expert on magicians.

REINER (*confused*): As I understand what you're trying to explain, Professor, your book is saying that there's a connection between the illusions of magicians and what happens to people in real life.

CAESAR: You got it, fella.

REINER: Can you give me an example?

CAESAR: You vant an example of great illusionary power? . . .

Hans Schnorkel . . . a Frenchman. He vas vorking on a trick mit a shark. So he got this shark . . . a two-thousand-pound tiger shark . . . und he put that shark in a tank mit over a million gallons of sea water. . . . Und then he stood on the side of the tank und he had himself handcuffed, behind his back. . . . There he vas, handcuffed mit just a bathing suit. . . . Und then, Hans threw himself into the tank mit the shark. . . . As soon as Hans hit the water, the shark spun around und started svimming slowly, slowly toward Hans. Und Hans, he just stood there in the tank und looked the shark right in the eye. . . . Und the shark just slowly stopped und looked Hans right back in the eye. . . . Und then, all of a sudden, the shark just rolled right over on his belly . . . and ate 'im.

REINER (*incredulous*): He *ate* him? What kind of an illusion is that?

CAESAR: It's a very good illusion. . . . But you gotta do it right. You see, don't start off rehearsing mit a shark. You start with a guppy, a goldfish, a nice herring, a piece of salmon is not bad. . . . Don't get crazy mit a shark right away.

REINER: That's an interesting story, Professor, but how does it apply to real life?

CAESAR: How? You can't see? You don't make the connection?

REINER: Sorry, Professor . . . I don't.

CAESAR: If you start out too big, you could let yourself be eaten up.

# 1

# Do I Want to Live, or Do I Want to Die?

When you're a drunk and a pill addict—as I was for most of my adult years—there comes a split second in your life when you have to make a fateful decision:

Do I want to live, or do I want to die?

For me, that split second came on the night of May 22, 1978.

I was at the Hotel Regina in Regina, Saskatchewan, where I had been booked to do the play *Last of the Red Hot Lovers* in the hotel's dining room. The booking was for six weeks. It was opening night, and I had just managed to stagger through the first act. Although I had done the play about a thousand times before and had long since memorized it, I couldn't remember my lines. I didn't even know where I was supposed to stand or sit. It was the first time this had ever happened to me. I kept missing cues and was causing chaos among the fine local Canadian actresses who had been hired as my supporting cast.

When the act ended, I lurched off the stage and went to my dressing room, a converted pantry just off the kitchen. I used to have an entourage of a dozen or more people waiting for me in my dressing room; the only one who was there now was Henry, one of the hotel's busboys, who had been assigned to me as my valet, or "dresser." Henry said, "What's wrong, Mr. Caesar?" I didn't answer. I just collapsed on my ratty little worn and stained couch.

And I thought.

Drunks think backward; they have no future and they can't cope with the present.

So, befuddled as I was, my mind was able to go back to many of the events—both good and bad—that had brought me to this point: I knew that the moment of decision was fast approaching.

Maybe I was trying to stave off my moment of truth—as I had done so many times before—by first recalling the Glory Years, when, as someone else once put it, there was too much, too soon. I remembered "Your Show of Shows" and "Caesar's Hour" in the early days of television in the 1950s. I was not yet thirty years old and was making a million dollars a year. For nine seasons, thirty-nine weeks a season, nearly everyone in the United States with a TV set would stay home on Saturday night to watch our live performances. Critics compared our work with the best plays on Broadway, which had been months in the making.

I remembered the fun and excitement of the five days in the writers' room that preceded each show. We started every Monday with absolutely nothing, and ended with a complete show. What a collection of talent! Show business has not seen the like of it—before or since. Sitting in that room with me, tossing ideas around like paper airplanes, were such geniuses as Neil Simon, Mel Brooks, Woody Allen, and Larry Gelbart, now among the top playwrights and movie creators in the entire world. I traded ideas with them and the others, perched in a special gold chair given to me by Larry Gelbart.

"We were a bunch of baby wolves," said Gelbart, "fighting to win the favor of Sid, the Papa Wolf." And fight they did. Chunks of plaster were knocked out of the walls; the draperies were ripped to shreds; Mel Brooks frequently was hanged in effigy by the others. But enormous creativity and fresh humor constantly bubbled in that room.

Someone tapped on the door. Henry, my busboy-turned-valet, looked at me anxiously. "I've got to get you ready to go back onstage, Mr. Caesar," he said.

"I'll be with you in a few minutes," I mumbled. Nausea now was beginning to grip my guts: my thoughts were now turning to how the Glory Years had subtly overlapped into the Dark Years.

I remembered the booze after each rehearsal, after each show—a relaxant, I thought, to ease the tension. My feelings of guilt, my gnawing self-doubts that I was worthy of the adulation, produced a constant fear that the gift would be taken away as suddenly and mysteriously as it had been bestowed on me. A fifth of Scotch at a time soon became two fifths. Then came the barbiturates and the tranquilizers the doctors gave me to wean me from the booze—except that I took the pills by the handful and washed them down *with* the booze. God, the vomiting, the fits of mindless violence that overcame me—ripping sinks out of walls, trying to throw Mel Brooks out of an eighteenth-story window . . . and the paranoia. Everyone was out to destroy me.

I remembered the cancellation of "Caesar's Hour" in 1958. In my mind, Robert Kintner, the president of NBC, was out to destroy me. I remembered *Little Me*, my last big show on Broadway, written by my old colleague Neil Simon. The show was a hit and I was a hit. I was playing seven roles, but I was convinced that the people were coming to see a dancer named Sven Svenson, not me . . . and that Svenson was out to destroy me.

I remembered how I slipped further into darkness. I kept working in films, on the stage, and in television—but I wasn't really there. It was like a twenty-year blackout. I'd even lost an entire continent. In 1976, I flew to Australia to make a movie called *Barnaby and Me* for director Norman Panama. When I got on the plane, I took my usual ration of pills and booze and passed out completely. When the plane made its stop in New Zealand, they couldn't wake me up. They rushed me to the hospital, thinking I'd had a stroke or a heart attack. It was an old habit of mine.

They sent for my wife, Florence. It was an old habit of hers.

Later, Florence told me how beautiful it had been in Australia. I just looked at her blankly. I could recall nothing about the country or the picture I'd done there. I saw *Barnaby and Me* in 1981, as part of a benefit for the Los Angeles Zoo. It was like watching another actor in a movie I knew absolutely nothing about.

Someone was at the dressing-room door yelling to Henry, "Get his ass out here. The second act is ready to begin." Henry tried to lift me off the couch, but I was too big for him.

Dear Florence, I thought, my faithful wife since we both were twenty years old. What a heroine in the classic mold! She'd held the family together for all these years, miraculously raising our three children so that they all were bright and normal and didn't hate their father too much. Dear Florence, never once leaving me, even at my worst, and always there when I needed her—like the time in New Zealand. She once threatened to write a book about me called *I Remember Monster*. So many people told her she deserved a chestful of medals that I actually gave her a chest, full of medals from a pawnshop.

What was it Florence had said to me before I'd left for Regina? "I've always been there with you before, but not this time. You've got to do a lot of thinking, alone, about this slow suicide you seem determined to commit."

By now, there was turmoil outside my dressing-room door. People were yelling; I could hear the overture being played over and over again.

I sat up and said to Henry, "Tell them I'm too sick to do the second act. And get me Dr. LeBlond, the hotel's doctor."

The noise outside subsided. Dr. LeBlond came in. He was a dapper, graying man in his fifties.

I was surprisingly calm. I said to Dr. LeBlond, "This is it. I want to live. Take me to the hospital."

Then I wasn't so calm anymore. I said, "Help me . . . please help me. . . ."

# 2
# No Hands on the Carriage

I had been in many hospitals before. It was always: "Dry out and go home, and keep in touch with your doctor. Dry out and go home, and we'll make sure the press doesn't hear about this."

But this time, in Regina General Hospital, province of Saskatchewan, Dominion of Canada, it was different. This time I *wanted* to be cured, and Dr. LeBlond and the others seemed to know it. It was my first tiny step in a long process of personal renewal, which didn't reach some realization until two years later in Paris. I know now that it is a process that will *never* end for the rest of my life.

The first thing they did at Regina General was to take me off all medication. They wouldn't even let me have my vitamin pills. I went through the withdrawal symptoms of years of alcohol and drug damage, unable to sleep for a week. I just paced up and down, up and down in my room, with the nurses constantly peering in at me.

In the quiet night hours of the hospital, I had plenty of time to begin the painful and endless process of puzzling out how it all started—and how it all went wrong.

It started in the rough factory town of Yonkers, New York, on the Hudson River, just north of New York City. That's where I was born, on September 8, 1922. They tell me it was a bleak day. Me, I don't remember. My father owned a luncheonette (known in the vernacular of the time as "a greasy spoon," "a one-arm joint"), which catered to the area's factory workers. After the heavy noontime business, he had to make his way through the rain to see me and my mother at the hospital. He disliked leaving the little restaurant solely in the charge of my eighteen-year-old brother, Abe, as the short-order cook, and my ten-year-old brother, Dave, as the cashier.

My father, Max, was a powerful, heavyset man like my brothers. He was very proud and stern, and imbued with the work ethic of the post–World War I immigrant population, which admirably—and sometimes not so admirably—meant getting ahead in life at all costs. He came from Poland, and God knows what the family name really was (Kaiser? Saiserovich?), but Caesar was the name bestowed on him by the immigration officer at Ellis Island. Those immigration officers played a lot of jokes with names on those innocent, non-English-speaking refugees from eastern Europe. The name Caesar seemed to be one of their favorite jokes. There were a lot of newly arrived Jewish Caesars in New York, among them a famous songwriter, Irving Caesar.

# Where Have I Been?

My mother, Ida, a tall, beautiful woman, came from Russia. She was much younger than my father, who was nearly fifty when I was born. I was what they called a "makeup child," meaning, I assume, that they were mad at each other for a long time, then made up, and I was the result. First they had had my brother, Abe, eighteen years earlier; then Milton, who died of meningitis; then Dave; and, ten years later, me. I was an infant in a family of giants. In addition to my very large parents, Abe was six feet four and weighed 260 pounds. Even Dave, my closest sibling, was well over six feet before he reached his teens.

I never knew how and when my father and mother met. In those days, the parents of people of our background didn't talk about romance or falling in love. They just got married and then they *were* married. My father did drop a few details about how he made his living when he arrived here as an immigrant boy. At first, he worked as a "Shabbes goy," turning on lights and stoves for more observant Jews who did not perform such functions on the Sabbath. The word *goy* means "Gentile," but for a fee of one dollar per household, he did not let his heritage stand in his way.

My father also came up with another interesting way of making a buck. For fifty cents a day, he'd break in a pair of new shoes for you simply by walking around in them. Since his feet were larger than those of most of his customers, it was a painful but lucrative profession. He got a lot of clients because of his rapid service; he couldn't stand wearing the shoes for more than a couple of days, and his big feet stretched the leather in the shoes in no time.

Later, my father entered into a partnership with his older brother, Joe, and these more exotic ways of making a living were forgotten when they opened the first of many luncheonettes they were to own. By the time I was born, my father had his own cafeteria, the St. Clair Buffet Lunch, with seventy-five rooms for rent upstairs. Rooms without windows cost fifty cents a night. Rooms with a window and fire escape were seventy-five cents. The fire escape was a rope tied to the radiator.

Actually, we were fairly well off when I was a child, so I can't blame poverty for my grown-up problems later on. I can't even fall back on the usual excuse of blaming my parents. I loved them very much and they loved *me* very much—but not very well. They did the best they could to "provide," which was the catchword of the day. That meant running the St. Clair Buffet Lunch twenty-four hours a day and leaving little Sidney mostly in the care of my preadolescent brother, Dave.

My very earliest memory is of one time when Dave was looking after me. I couldn't have been more than six months old. He had me outside our house at 27 Hawthorne Avenue. I was in my carriage. Yonkers is a hilly city and Hawthorne Avenue is a very steep street.

What I remember is that I was comfortable in the carriage, with Dave's nice, safe hands on the push-bar. To my infant mind, those hands represented love and protection. But then, suddenly, the hands were gone. Dave, a ten-year-old boy bored with babysitting, had concocted a little game to amuse himself. I learned later that he had tied a rope to the carriage and let me roll down the hill, to the very end of the length of the rope. He did it over and over again. It amused him, but it apparently terrified *me*. The scene comes back to me to this very day—especially at times when *other* loving, protective hands are suddenly removed without explanation.

My father had loving, protective hands and was the symbol

of strength in our family, but I hardly ever saw him when I was a baby. In order to undercut the competition in the luncheonette business by a few pennies, he used to get up at two o'clock in the morning and make the long drive to the produce market in downtown New York to be there when it opened at 4:00 A.M. I somehow remember—perhaps from later observation—that he fortified himself against the early-morning cold by drinking a tumbler of whiskey laced with a couple of spoons of hot red pepper. He'd get back with his truckful of vegetables at about five-thirty, just in time to serve breakfast to the factory workers coming to the luncheonette. Breakfast was over by eight o'clock. Then came preparation for lunch. Then dinner. He'd come home from the luncheonette after Dave took over at 6:00 P.M., but my mother would have me in bed soon after that. My father himself would be asleep by nine. To make up for his inability to give me more time and attention, he did what most other immigrant Yonkers parents did: he bought me a lot of *things*.

My beautiful mother, too, did the best she could and the best she knew how. Everyone else in the family went off to eat breakfast at the luncheonette, but she insisted on staying home to make breakfast for me, the baby. That was the best time, as she fussed over me and fed me my oatmeal, and sometimes even kissed me and sang the song " Mein Kind." I still remember her tall, strong body and her dark, bobbed hair. But then she was gone, too, and Dave took over. She was needed at the cafeteria for lunch, the busiest time of the day, when workers poured out of the telephone company building, the Otis Elevator factory, the sugar refinery, and the hat company.

As I grew older, I learned more about this mysterious world that gobbled up my family and took them away from me every day. I went to school nearby at P.S. 10 and I could walk over to the St. Clair Buffet Lunch. I would help out by clearing a few dishes from the tables, but mostly I would just be fascinated by the customers. Nearly all of them were young, single immigrants who would segregate into groups speaking Italian, Russian, Hungarian, Polish, French, Spanish, Lithuanian, and even Bulgarian. I would go from table to table, listening to the sounds. I learned how to mimic them, sounding as if I actually were speaking their language. They weren't offended.

The first time I tried it out, I went over to a table of Italians. I was so small that my head was barely above the table as I rattled away in my Italian double-talk. When I began, they all smiled happily at me as if to say, "Hey, this kid is one of our own." Then they cocked their heads, listened carefully and looked at one another, jabbering away. They must have been asking, "What's he saying? What's he saying?" Finally they realized what I was up to and they roared with laughter, slapping me on the back and poking each other in the ribs. One of them asked, in English, "Hey, kid, can you speaka Polack lika that, too?" When I said yes, he sent me to do my act at a nearby table of Poles. Before it was over, the whole place was breaking up and it was the beginning of a comic device that helped me earn millions later on.

I soon found out that my mimicry could get the attention of my father and mother and make them laugh, too. Mel Tolkin (the head writer on "Your Show of Shows" and "Caesar's Hour," and later one of the key writers of "All in the Family") has an interesting theory. He says, "Nearly all good comedians were either an only child or the youngest child of very busy parents. As kids, they had to be funny in order to compete for attention and love."

Where Have I Been?

I guess that's what I was doing at the St. Clair Buffet Lunch and at 27 Hawthorne Avenue.

As I got a little older, I became more and more aware of my parents' life patterns. My father, along with working so hard, still managed to have some spare diversions. He was friendly with the few Jewish businessmen in town and occasionally would play poker or pinochle with them—or meet them at the tobacco store to buy cigars, the symbol of affluence in immigrant society. Then, as in their previous lives in Europe, there was the *shul* as the center of community life. Ours was the Agudath Achim Synagogue. My father was not a religious man, but he was always there for the important holidays. He had his regular pew and we were expected to join him. The most important men in the *shul* were two prosperous merchants named Collins (the name was the result of another of those tricks of the immigration officers) and Duman. Whenever I did anything wrong, he was always afraid of "what the Collinses and the Dumans would think."

My father would hit me occasionally, usually as the consequence of my doing something he thought would stimulate unfavorable thoughts in the minds of the Collinses and the Dumans. On one Yom Kippur, for example, I was excused from the *shul* for a while during the part of the service when survivors mourn the dead. It was World Series time, a perennial unfortunate conflict with the High Holy Days. I wandered over to Herald Square, where the *Yonkers Herald-Statesman* had a huge electric board detailing the play-by-play progress of the action between the Philadelphia Athletics and the St. Louis Cardinals. I became so engrossed in the game that I was a half hour late getting back to *shul*. My father took me outside, walloped me, and asked the inevitable question, "What will the Collinses and the Dumans think?"

When I was a bit older, my brother Dave took me down to Harlem to see Ella Fitzgerald perform. It was the eve of Rosh Hashanah, the Jewish New Year. The subway and bus system broke down that night and we didn't get home until morning—long after we were supposed to be in *shul*. I had gotten undressed to change into my synagogue clothes, when I heard the front door go *thrump*. From the way the smashing sound bounced through the house, I knew it was my father. I put on my shoes and socks and took off—naked. Dave wasn't so lucky. He was cornered in the bathroom and got belted pretty good—even though he was already six feet three and weighed 280 pounds.

In the nonreligious area, the greatest excitement came when my father and mother made occasional Sunday trips to the Lower East Side in New York. They always took me with them. There were no expressways then, so the drive was an arduous one—through the hilly streets of Yonkers, down Broadway from Washington Heights to mid-Manhattan, and then down Park Avenue the rest of the way. It took about two hours.

The routine was always the same. We'd drop my mother off at Hester Street to do her shopping for clothes and items for the house. It always amazed us to watch her enter one shop and then surface again from another shop a block away and across the street. Apparently there was a warren of tunnels from one place to another under the pavement. She never explained.

While Mother was shopping, my father and I went to the Russian steam baths on St. Mark's Place. It was explained to me that one of the rites of manhood was to be able to withstand the heat on the top shelf closest to the steam, turning over only four times. I, of course, was nowhere near being able to effect such a glorious accomplishment.

Where Have I Been?

After the baths, we would meet my mother at some fancy Lower East Side restaurant like Moskowitz and Lupowitz. My mother would be glowing over the treasure trove of items she had bought at bargain prices, and my father would be mellow and tell stories about his earliest days in the United States. After dinner we'd go to a movie at Loew's Delancey. Those were the fun days of my childhood, and I doubted if even the Collinses and the Dumans enjoyed anything like it.

# 3
# Chopped Liver on the Mouthpiece

The depression struck in 1929, when I was seven. Even at that young age I was aware of its effects on my father and mother. Somehow my father was no longer as vigorous and powerful as he had been, and it scared me—especially when he was hesitant about going to *shul* because of his loss of pride at no longer being able to make donations that would keep up with the Collinses and the Dumans.

But he did continue to go to *shul*, where he learned that even the Collinses and the Dumans had cut their donations; and he did manage to hang on to the St. Clair Buffet Lunch, for a while. We eventually had to give up the house on Hawthorne Avenue, however, and we moved into six of the tiny hotel rooms above the restaurant. By that time I was playing the saxophone, and because of my constant practicing on the instrument, there was a switch in the popularity of the other sixty-nine rooms that were rented out to paying guests. Now, there was more of a demand for the fifty-cents-a-night rooms without windows than for the seventy-five-cents-a-night rooms with windows, through which the noise of the saxophone more easily penetrated.

My introduction to the saxophone was sheer chance. All Jewish kids in Yonkers were pressed by their parents to take music lessons, but usually it was the piano or the violin. That's what had happened with my two brothers. But one day my father came to me with a beat-up brass saxophone in his hands and said, "Some deadbeat moved out of his room without paying and left this behind. The cops said I could keep it if the deadbeat didn't come back for it in thirty days. So now it's thirty days, and it's yours."

"Where am I going to learn how to play this saxophone?" I asked.

He said, "I already looked into that. Over there in Tuckahoe, there is an orphans' home. They have there a music teacher who knows about the clarinet and the saxophone and all what they call wind instruments. He only charges fifty cents a lesson. Besides, the name of the place is the Hebrew National Home, so how could it be bad?"

I was now eleven and was quite adept at using the public transportation system. Two days a week, after school, I would take the Number Seven Yonkers trolley all the way to the end of the line, and then board a bus to the orphanage. The music teacher there was a nice man in his forties who taught me well but who annoyed me because I always knew what he had eaten for lunch. He made me aware of that by taking my saxophone, whenever I made a mistake, and putting my mouthpiece between his lips to play a passage for me the way it *should* have been played. Then, when I had to play the passage again, I could taste his entire lunch on the mouth-piece—onions with chopped liver, cabbage soup, a little *ge-dempte brust*. . . . Sometimes I didn't like what he ate. Once I said, "Could you use a little less salt, please?" He didn't know what I was talking about, but even if he had, he wouldn't have laughed. He was not what you would call a good audience.

My problem with his eating habits ended abruptly one snowy winter day when I got off the bus across the street from the Home and a delivery truck slid into me as I stepped off the curb. I was knocked down, but the saxophone took the brunt of the blow. It wasn't smashed, but it came apart and was in pieces all over the street. People rushed out of the Home and carried me to the infirmary. They checked me for broken bones, but I didn't have anything more serious than some very black-and-blue bruises. They kept asking me how I felt and I kept asking them about the saxophone. I was thinking, "If that saxophone is smashed, boy, am I going to get it."

Both the saxophone and I ended up OK, but when I got home, my mother stepped in and made the decision that should have been made long ago. She said to my father, "A boy has to go all the way to Tuckahoe to take music lessons and get hit by a truck? Somewhere, in all Yonkers, in the middle of a depression, there's gotta be another music teacher who gives saxophone lessons for the same fifty cents?" There was—and my brother Abe found him.

So my lessons continued, and so did my formal education

in the Yonkers school system. I finished P.S. 10 and went to Benjamin Franklin Junior High School in the immigrant section of town. No day there was complete without a big fistfight after school. Fighting was like an extracurricular activity. As soon as the bell rang at three o'clock, it was take off the coat, tell someone "Let's go," and whang, a fight. It was part of the system. One day you'd fight a guy and the next day you'd be helping him fight someone else. There was only one guy who was genuinely mad at me. That was Joey Leffler, and he beat the hell out of me. Why, I'll never know. Finally, my mother went to the board of education and petitioned them to transfer me to Hawthorne Junior High School, which was known as the rich kids' school. It was very classy there— only one fight a week. And the fights were a lot more polite: "You want to put your books down? I'll wait for you."

By the time I got to Hawthorne, I was pretty good with the sax, so I got together with five other kids and we formed a dance band. I had to find some way of making a buck to help out at home because things were going so badly financially for the family. My father went bankrupt in 1935 and not only lost the St. Clair Buffet Lunch but also some land he had acquired in Yonkers and in Florida. He opened the Chambers Lunch in New York City and lost it, then the Main Lunch Bar back in Yonkers and lost it, and finally a novelty shop in Yonkers with my brother Dave operating a two-dollar bookie parlor in the back room. If someone wanted to bet ten dollars on a horse, the action was too much for Dave to handle and he had to lay it off with another bookie.

I tried to help out with the earnings I made with the band at school. We did dances and weddings, but the whole band would play for a dollar fifty, to be split up by six guys. When I graduated from Hawthorne Junior High and went to Yonkers

High School, it looked like the promised land for my musician's income. There were kids there—Mike Dooley, Mike Cifficello—who had bands that they booked all over the city, and it was possible to make three to five dollars a week per *man*. I eventually ended up with Mike Cifficello's Swingtime Six, but first there was a crisis, not of my own making.

It happened on the first day of school, when I was just starting the tenth grade at Yonkers High. The football coach saw me walking across the schoolyard. He came up to me and said, "Oh, boy, you're six feet and over two hundred pounds, and you're going to play tackle for me."

I said, "I don't want to play tackle."

He said, "Why not? It's good for your character, and besides it will excuse you from gym classes."

I said, "But I'm a musician. It might hurt my lip, and that would cost me a dollar fifty a night."

The coach said, "Not to worry. Just hold your lips like this." And he pulled his lips tight across his teeth, like a guy who had just eaten a lemon.

He was very persuasive, so I came out for the first practice. They gave me a uniform, shoulder pads, and one of those old-fashioned leather helmets. They didn't know from face-masks in those days. We did calisthenics and we went through the fundamentals of line play. Then the coach got us down on our hands for a single play from scrimmage. I was supposed to block. The quarterback called the play and wham, I was flat on my back on the grass with a bloody nose and a split lip. I got up and said, "Thank you, lots of luck, it was nice knowing you, here's your uniform back, good-bye." That was the beginning and the end of my entire football career.

The split lip healed, and that's when I became a member of Mike Cifficello's Swingtime Six. We not only played at school but also at restaurants and bars all over Yonkers. These were joints that could have had a sign outside: "Dining, Dancing, Fighting." We memorized "The Star-Spangled Banner" immediately. The minute we heard someone say "Fuck you" in Italian, Russian, German, Hungarian, Polish, Lithuanian, or even Bulgarian, it was a cue for us to stop whatever we were playing and bring everyone to attention with the national anthem, before the real fighting could get started. Sometimes it worked; sometimes it didn't.

By my senior year at Yonkers High, we were regulars at a restaurant called Villanova. Mike Cifficello had graduated by now and was a milkman, but he still kept the band together because his milk route didn't begin until after we stopped playing. He was a genius at getting bookings for us. I was making a steady six dollars a week now. I was still living with my parents, of course, and I "gave to the house," as it was called then. I'd turn over all my money to my mother and keep fifty cents for myself. Once, I kept a dollar and felt guilty.

When I graduated in 1939, I had a difficult decision to make. The money I was contributing wasn't enough, and I didn't like the way things were going at home. My father was just a shell of his former self. He was a very proud man brought down by economic stress. He no longer was forceful. He felt defeated. I was beginning to feel that *I* had to go through the same thing; otherwise I wouldn't be a man. It was dangerous thinking, which would continue to surface—in different forms—later in my life.

I decided to head south to New York City. There was a union there, the American Federation of Musicians, and I heard that a good saxophone player could make as much as twenty dollars a week.

# 4

# A Concerto, or a Tomato in the Face?

I was only sixteen years old and I was a little scared when I took the subway from Van Cortlandt Park all the way down to Times Square. I went in to see the people at Local 802 of the musicians union and they were very nice to me. I was so big that they thought I was at least twenty, but they said I couldn't become a member until I had lived in the city as a resident for six months. They recommended a boardinghouse run by a Mrs. Fuchs, who was sort of a housemother for aspiring young musicians.

I went over to see Mrs. Fuchs at her building at Fiftieth

Street and Eighth Avenue, just across the street from the old Madison Square Garden. She was a nice middle-aged German lady. Somehow *she* knew I was only sixteen and she took a liking to me right away. She said I could have a room for four dollars a week. Meals would be thirty cents for breakfast, forty cents for lunch, and fifty cents for dinner. She told me I could get a job as an usher in a movie theater, which would more than cover the room and board. She said, "If you were blond and looked like a West Point cadet, the Radio City Music Hall would take you, but for your type, I think better the Capitol Theater just down the block."

The Capitol took me. In those days, Broadway movie houses hired ushers who would look as if they were guarding Buckingham Palace. I was tall enough and broad enough to meet the requirements. I was amazed at the salary: fifteen dollars a week.

I went home to Yonkers to pack my suitcase. All this news did not sit well with my mother, even though she knew I'd now be able to "give more to the house." She was sure that Mrs. Fuchs would starve me. To make her point, she served me a huge farewell supper of mushroom-and-barley soup, brisket of beef, potatoes, and string beans. In my attempts to make everyone in the family laugh, one of my most successful routines always had been about the duel I waged with my mother at every meal. I told how I carefully arranged my plate so that meat, potatoes, and vegetables would come out even—and how my mother would always louse up my careful planning by slapping an extra portion of something on the plate at the last minute. *This* night she slapped so much extra on the plate that it wouldn't have come out even—even if I stayed until midnight.

She was crying when I said good-bye to her. You'd think

24

I had been sentenced to Siberia, when actually I'd be home in less than a week, on my first day off. I felt terrible, but at the same time I had a feeling of excitement about what lay ahead.

New York was fun in September of 1939. War had broken out in Europe, but it all seemed so far away that it would never touch us. There were four other young musicians staying at Mrs. Fuchs's boardinghouse and we had wonderful talks about Benny Goodman and Harry James, not Churchill and Hitler. We had impromptu jam sessions. Fortunately, they did not annoy Mrs. Fuchs, who was used to it. Also, she was a little deaf. She was so nice that the one thing I did worry about was eating her out of house and home. Her mealtime portions were *not* as big as my mother's, and since I was giving so much to the house at Yonkers, I frequently was too broke to avail myself of the fifty-cent dinner. So I did a lot of raiding of the icebox. Because I didn't want to take advantage of Mrs. Fuchs, I made the cheapest sandwich possible: catsup between two slices of bread. Also, I'd go to the Automat and make tomato soup out of free boiling water (available for tea) and free catsup (from the bottle set out on every table). Mrs. Fuchs affectionately called me Little Perkel, which means "little pig" in German.

At the Capitol Theater, the usher's job was routine—mostly standing around and looking formidable. But when the weather turned cold in November, a doorman quit to seek warmer employment, and I rocketed up to the post of doorman—with a three-dollar-a-week raise—simply because I was the only usher who fit the departing guy's overcoat.

It was a whole new world. The Capitol, being a very fancy place showing only first-run MGM movies, forbade its doormen to speak to the public unless spoken to. We did not have to bark out the time of the next show, as in lesser movie palaces. We just stood there, haughty as possible. I was *so* haughty that a lot of people gave me a ten-cent tip just for opening the door, which I was supposed to do anyway. Occasionally, an MGM movie star, like Lana Turner or Claire Trevor, would show up. It was my job to escort her to the elevator (we didn't want her shoes to get dirty walking up the stairs) and then take her directly to one of the $1.25 divans in the loge.

To the public, I must have looked like a field marshal pacing his command post. A couple would approach me timidly and ask, "Excuse me, sir, but do we have time for a sandwich before the show starts?" I was already working out comic routines in my head, just like I used to do at home. I'd say, "That depends on whether you have a fast sandwich or a slow sandwich. A fast sandwich is like bacon and tomato, where they already have the bacon made up. A slow sandwich is like pastrami, where you have to wait around for them to slice the meat." I'd look at my watch and say, "In your case, you couldn't get away with anything slower than egg salad or tuna fish." I'd touch my fingers to my cap, and they'd thank me and give me a dime tip.

On the coldest day of the year, who should pull up in front of the theater but my mother, driven by my brother Dave in his old Chrysler. She had brought me a warm muffler and a Thermos of hot soup. I kept doing my work while sipping the soup and chatting with Dave and my mother. Herman Landwehr, the theater manager, came running out, asking, "What the hell is going on here?" I said, "A mother brings soup all the way from Yonkers. What am I going to do—tell her to go away?" Landwehr retreated in confusion and told that story at parties for years.

My hours as a doorman were from 10:00 A.M. to 1:00 P.M.,

and from 4:00 P.M. to 8:30 P.M. That gave me three hours each day, from one to four, to keep up with my music studies. By now I was convinced the saxophone could be played as a serious musical instrument, especially after I heard a record of *Concertino da camera* by composer Jacques Ibert, a concerto for saxophone played by Marcel Mulé and the Paris Conservatory Orchestra. So I studied with Frank Chase of the NBC Symphony in his little studio at Fiftieth Street and Sixth Avenue. I also sneaked into the Juilliard School of Music, with a pencil behind my ear like a regular student, and audited courses in harmony, theory, and orchestration. I'd practice at Mrs. Fuchs's whenever she assured me the other boarders were not asleep.

Apparently, I impressed one of the other musicians at Mrs. Fuchs's, because as soon as my six months of residency were up and I could join the union, he got me a booking with the Shep Fields orchestra, which then consisted almost entirely of saxophones. I was only seventeen years old. My days as a movie doorman were over. I was sure now that I'd go on to France to study with the greatest saxophonist in the world, Marcel Mulé.

It didn't work out that way.

First of all, there was the war. I was paying more attention to it now. The Nazis had blitzkrieged their way through Poland; I had seen newsreels of the Japanese rape of Nanking; more and more refugee Jews were coming to the United States with their horror stories of what was going on in Europe. Maybe I was more sensitive than most seventeen-year-olds, but I knew instinctively that this war was going to be a long-haul thing. That meant no studying in Paris because the Germans could attack France at any time. It also meant that the United States probably would soon have a draft, and at my age, I would be one of the first to be called up. So I decided to get as much out of life as I could, for as long as I could, and not make any long-term commitments.

If I hadn't taken that attitude, I might have ended up permanently with the Shep Fields orchestra—and my career never would have gone in the direction it did.

I spent only two weeks with Fields, but it was the most exciting period of my life until then. I made forty-five dollars a week, which seemed like a fortune to me. I was totally accepted as a fine saxophone player by Fields and the other musicians, who went out of their way to help the kid from Yonkers. We played nightly at the Edison Hotel on Broadway, and we recorded two Shep Fields records while I was with the band. It was an interesting musical combination: nine saxophones and four rhythm instruments. Shep was still evolving variations on the "Rippling Rhythm" concept he had invented.

When the two weeks were up, Shep said to me, "I'm going on the road, kid, and you fit in so well that I want you to come with the band permanently."

What I said then really tore me up, but I knew I was doing the right thing. I told him, "Mr. Fields, there's nothing I'd like better, but we're going to get into this war and I'm going to be drafted."

He said, "What are you going to do in the meantime?"

I said, "Have as much fun as I can."

He shrugged and said, "OK, if you want to be a shmuck, so be a shmuck." And that was that.

Actually, I still had ideas of becoming a serious musician. My teacher, Frank Chase, kept telling me I was a star student, and I wanted him to teach me the clarinet, the oboe, the flute, and the bassoon—all of which *he* played for Arturo Toscanini and André Kostelanetz.

But I was still living at Mrs. Fuchs's boardinghouse and

was broke again. I got pick-up jobs playing the saxophone with little bands wherever I could. I didn't even have a decent saxophone, let alone a clarinet, oboe, flute, or bassoon. One day when I came to his studio, Frank Chase pulled out the most beautiful gold-plated saxophone I had ever seen. It was a Selma, the best. He said, "I just picked this up and you can have it for a hundred-and-fifteen dollars." I looked at that magnificent instrument and my tongue hung out. I said, "Let me go home and talk to my father, and I'll see what I can do."

I took the subway up to Yonkers and told my father about the beautiful Selma saxophone. He looked at me with the saddest look I can remember. "There's nothing I wouldn't give you if I could," he said, "but where am *I* going to come up with a hundred-and-fifteen dollars?" I went back to Frank Chase and told him I didn't have the money for the Selma. He said, "Borrow the money." I said, "On *what*?" I think it was the first time he actually realized how poor I was. He said, "I'll have to sell the Selma to someone else, but I think I'll have to get you some jobs."

He did. He lined up work for me with the Claude Thornhill and Charlie Spivak bands at the Glen Island Casino. Six months later I could have afforded Frank's Selma. I finally was able to buy a Selma of my own—which I still have—but it never has been able to compare with that gold-plated beauty I could have owned in 1940.

It's funny how such minor incidents sometimes play a larger role in your life. I don't know whether that was the case with me, but after I couldn't buy the gold-plated Selma, my life seemed to take a different turn. I continued as a musician; it was the only way I knew how to make a living. But even as I went off in Art Mooney's Band, say, on such gigs as playing the Pick Ohio Hotel in Youngstown, Ohio, with its famous "all-stainless-steel dance floor," my mind was not so much on oboes and Jacques Ibert's concertino for saxophone anymore. Instead, I was looking forward to my summers, when I'd always play with a little band at some Catskill Mountain resort hotel, and—on the side—help out the resident comic with some of the gags and comedy inventions I used to come up with at home to catch the attention of my parents and brothers.

This parallel interest of mine had begun several years before, when I was still a sophomore in high school and playing with Mike Cifficello's Swingtime Six. Cifficello got us a summer booking at the Anderson Hotel in Monticello, New York. It was my very first time away from home. The comedian at the Anderson was Jackie Michaels, whose training, as in most such cases, was in burlesque. Michaels needed a stooge for his routines and with no straight man on the tight payroll, who could be better for him than a big, thunky kid named Sid Caesar, who played the saxophone in the hotel band?

A typical Jackie Michaels routine went like this:

MICHAELS (*to assistant*): What do I have in my hand, an egg or a tomato?
ASSISTANT: An egg.
MICHAELS (*smashing tomato into assistant's face*): You're wrong. It's a tomato.

I didn't really mind this sort of thing. In fact, it was a lot of fun for a fourteen-year-old and it made me popular with the girl guests at the hotel, who became much more aware of me than if I had just been sitting there playing the saxophone.

30

But, at the same time, it made me wonder. Why did so much comedy of that day depend on the degradation of another human being? Why did most of the laughs seem to come from throwing a pie in someone's face or squirting him with a seltzer bottle? Certainly there was another way. Even as a kid at home and in my father's restaurant, I had people in hysterics simply by mimicking the funny things I saw in *real* life. I remembered how I found humor in the ritual of men going to the steam baths, in women searching for a certain type of herring in the delicatessen, even in the daily duel between me and my mother as she thwarted me in my attempts to have the foods on my dinner plate come out even.

In the summer of 1939—just before I went to New York to Mrs. Fuchs and the Capitol Theater—I had another summer job playing the saxophone at Vacationland in Swan Lake in the Catskills. The so-called social director at this hotel was Don Appel. The Catskill-resort social director in those days was a very important man. He was a promoter, who, in addition to keeping the guests diverted with organized games and making-friends diversions, also had the responsibility for putting the hotel's entertainment package together. After the hotel hired him, sometime in the spring, he had to assemble the personnel to keep the guests occupied at night in the hotel's dancehall-theater, usually called the Casino and pronounced "casina." By the time the resort opened, just before the Fourth of July, the social director was expected to have hired a staff consisting, at the minimum, of a comic, a straight man, a singer, and a dancer.

In 1939 Appel had assembled such a package for Vacationland. I was not part of it because I was simply the saxophonist with the band, which had been hired separately by the hotel. However, as I had done previously in these summer-musician jobs, I immediately offered to help out with the sketches. I was even willing to take a tomato in the face again. Not having to pay me out of his budget, Appel was grateful and let me become a part-time performer.

Appel was a thoughtful, youngish man in his late twenties, who came from Brownsville in Brooklyn, where one of his neighbors and protégés was a very young Mel Brooks, then only about thirteen. Appel's ambition was to do serious theater, and, indeed, he later produced plays on Broadway for the great Yiddish comedienne Molly Picon. That summer at Vacationland he had more immediate worries. He had to stage an activity in the Casino every night of the week. Monday was bingo; Tuesday was dance night; Wednesday was a revue; Thursday was game night; Friday was a drama; Saturday was another revue. He needed all the bodies he could get to keep this schedule going and he used me all the time. For me, it was great experience, better than going to college. Drama night was especially exciting. We did plays and musicals like *Of Mice and Men, Pins and Needles,* and practically everything Clifford Odets ever wrote.

The only thing that continued to bother me was the quality of the comedy in the revues. I said to Appel, "Why do we just keep doing the old burlesque sketches? Let's make up some new stuff."

He could have told me to just play the saxophone in the band and keep my nose out of his business, but Appel was not that kind of man. He said to me mildly, "But we have all the sketches in the trunk."

I said, "I know that's the easiest thing to do, but these people mostly laugh at the old skits because they know them by heart and are just waiting for the punch line to come up. Why do just that? Let's start with two guys going into a bakery to shop, for example, and take it from there, making up funny situations that can happen in a real bakery. Who's going to kill you here? Let's try."

Appel thought about it for a long time. Then he said, "OK, let's try." We did. Some things worked and some things didn't. But people started coming over from other hotels to see our improvisations, and Appel finally conceded that we were on the right path. He particularly liked some stories I made up from my days in my father's luncheonette, using the foreign-language double-talk.

The following summer, 1940, I was back again at Vacationland playing the saxophone in the band and helping out Appel with more of the same stuff.

The summer after that, 1941, Appel moved to Kutscher's Hotel in Monticello, New York. This time he asked me to reverse my roles. Instead of playing the saxophone in the band and helping him out on the stage, he wanted me to be *the* comedian in his troupe and occasionally help out in the band. We now were developing a trunkful of *new* sketches, which we kept perfecting. I don't think we used a single old routine that summer.

When the season ended on Labor Day, 1941, I went back to New York to play in bands wherever I could. By now I was known as a good, competent saxophonist, and it wasn't too hard to find work. I didn't want anything steady. Military conscription was in effect, and I could have been drafted anytime. With Pearl Harbor, the situation became even more acute. My brother Abe was in the Coast Guard by then. He liked it, and I decided to enlist in that branch of the service. I was sworn in, but I was told I wouldn't have to report for active duty until after the summer. I didn't know what I was going to do until then.

Where Have I Been?

In the meantime, however, certain events were taking place, which I knew nothing about until later. I'll let my wife, Florence, tell that part of the story.

## Florence Caesar

*I had just finished my third year at Hunter College, and, as usual, I was going to spend the summer helping out at my uncle's hotel in the Catskills. My uncle was Meyer Arkin. The place he owned was the Avon Lodge in Woodridge, New York, one of the best hotels in "the mountains." The whole family worked there. I usually was in the office, but I was planning to get my teacher's certificate, so that summer of 1942, I also was going to get some experience with kids by being the hotel's governess.*

*But, before the season began, we had a problem. For years the entertainment at the lodge was handled by the Bernardi family—you know, the famous Bernardis from the Yiddish stage. Herschel Bernardi, who's now a very well known Broadway and TV actor, is one of them, but at the time he was too young to work at the lodge. The social directors for the past few years had been his older brother and sister, Jack and Fay Bernardi. Jack and Fay were asking for more money for the coming season, and my uncle wouldn't go along with their demands. So suddenly, with the Fourth of July coming up on us pretty fast, we had no entertainment staff.*

*You couldn't run a hotel in the Catskills without entertainment—especially a prestige place like the Avon Lodge—so my uncle called an emergency meeting of the family. He designated me and my cousin, Lillian Arkin, to come up with another social director. And fast.*

## A Concerto, or a Tomato in the Face?

*We started interviewing people who had done well at other hotels. One of them was Don Appel. I had heard a lot about how Don had turned things around at Vacationland and at Kutscher's, so he was one of the first we called in. Lillian and I liked him immediately. He was kind of scholarly and dignified and a lot different from your average social director. We offered him the job.*

*He said, "I'll take it, but with one proviso. There's a brilliant young comic who worked with me at the other hotels. He does stuff that's new and very funny. I want him to be included with me as part of the package. And, by the way, he also plays the saxophone."*

*I said, "How much would we have to pay him?"*

*Appel said, "He can't work for a penny less than two hundred dollars for the season. He needs the money. He's going into the service in October."*

*I said, "Well, two hundred for ten weeks seems a little high, but as long as he's going into the service, I guess it will be OK with my uncle."*

*Lillian and I shook hands with Appel on the deal.*

*I never even asked the young comedian's name.*

# 5

# Enter Florence,
# from Stage Left

Florence learned my name pretty fast.

Ordinarily I'm very shy when I'm in my own persona. It's different when I play some other character; I can hide behind that character and let *him* be brash and aggressive. Later, Larry Gelbart used to say that the toughest line he ever wrote for me was when I had to get up in front of a studio audience as just plain Sid Caesar and say, "Good evening, ladies and gentlemen. Welcome to the show." Larry maintains that one night he wrote forty versions of that line before I could get it right. That fear of being *me* isn't there anymore—ever since,

36

many years later, I finally "made friends with myself," as I call it.

But the fear definitely still was there when I first set eyes on Florence Levy after I arrived at the Avon Lodge in 1942—which is what makes it seem all that much more miraculous when I think back to what I did.

I saw her through the office window, from a walkway between two buildings, and I thought to myself, "Wow! That's the most beautiful girl I've ever seen." She was tall and willowy, about five nine, and she had silky pale blond hair pulled straight back over perfect features and the brightest, biggest blue-gray eyes. I had seen plenty of showgirls and singers when I played with the bands, but never anything like this. Looking through the window at her intelligent and ladylike movements, I could think of only one word: class.

Without a second's hesitation, I walked directly into the office and said to this stunning young woman, "Hello. I'm Sid Caesar."

She put out her hand and said, "I'm Florence Levy. I guess you're the young comedian Don Appel brought here with him."

I said, "That's who I am." She didn't seem to be very interested. But the next thing I said *did* catch her attention: "I have absolutely fallen in love."

I amazed myself with this unusual outburst of boldness—for me—but I didn't really mean it at the time. All I was looking for was a summer romance, which probably would fade in the fall—someone to dance with, to talk to. With a girl of Florence's type, sex was unthinkable. At nineteen, I was a very romantic young fellow and falling in love all the time. Not that I ever *did* anything. Until that point in my life, the only time I had ever been laid was when I was thirteen years old. It was then that my two much-older brothers said to me, "Today you are a man," and they took me to a whorehouse in Yonkers. I guess they thought it was kind of funny to do that, but for me it was a very upsetting experience. The beat-up old hooker said, "OK, let's go, sonny," and in a few seconds it was on, off, over, good-bye. I remember thinking to myself, "That's *it?* That's the whole mystery? You could have a woman next to you in bed the whole night, and that's all it would amount to?"

So, for the rest of my growing-up years, I observed the customs of the times in my relations with girls. Getting laid, that was already marriage. It was a big thing in those days to brush up against a tit with your elbow. A little squeeze of the ass, that was like going all the way.

With Florence, I can't say that I didn't let those thoughts intrude, but I immediately forced myself to put them out of my mind. Mostly we talked. We were two very earnest young people and we spent most of that wonderful summer discussing everything from F. Scott Fitzgerald to Leon Trotsky. Florence was nineteen then, like me, but she was much smarter than I was. She was a literature major in college, and she knew everything about books, plays, and films. Being just a high school graduate, I really couldn't keep up with her, but you don't realize things like that when you're a kid. You just go along with your instincts. She talked to me; I trusted her; I felt I wanted to be with her.

How did Florence feel about me? Let her tell you herself.

## Florence Caesar

*When I met Sid at the Avon Lodge that summer, the first thing I thought was that he was a very nice-looking guy. He wasn't my type. I liked older, more serious boys. But I figured that just for the summer, why not? Sid looked to me like he could be a lot of fun.*

*But then, when we started having our endless conversations, I began to realize he was a lot more serious and deep than I had thought. He knew wonderful things about classical music, and once, when we were alone in the Casino, he put a French record on the phonograph and played the entire* Concertino da camera *concerto on his saxophone from memory, with the symphony orchestra on the record backing him up. He knew about Bach and Vivaldi and Stravinsky.*

*He hadn't been to college, but it was obvious he was self-educated. He recited from Clifford Odets plays and could quote from John Steinbeck. Most of all, he had read an astonishing amount of history. It was his hobby. He could talk about the Napoleonic Wars, Julius Caesar's invasion of Gaul, and the complicated political events in Europe that led up to World War I.*

*Once, after I watched him doing a hilarious sketch in one of the revues in the Casino—something about a bashful teen-aged boy at his first dance—I asked him how one mind could think up such funny things and still get hooked on as serious a subject as history.*

*He said, "The background of a lot of comedy is history. If you study how people walked, how they ate, how they negotiated with each other, how they adopted status symbols in certain periods, you have the basis of a lot of good funny sketches."*

*The way he talked, I grew fonder and fonder of him. We came from different backgrounds, but after a while it didn't seem to matter. My father owned a printing business and I was so radical-chic that I used to march in the May Day parades and wave my banner defiantly at his store when we passed it. Sid's background, on the other hand, was the lunch-eonette in Yonkers and touring to places like the all-stainless-steel dance floor in Ohio. He was strictly nonpolitical. Still, we ended up having a lot in common.*

*When my mother and my aunt saw how much we were together, they said things like, "He's a very talented boy, but that doesn't mean he's going to have a great career," and "You should at least have a doctor." My father said, "A good businessman is even better than a doctor. With Sid, if you marry him, at least you'll have good-looking kids, but you're going to have to work all your life to support him."*

Florence and I weren't even thinking of marriage—yet. It was still a summer romance, but a very satisfactory one. For me, it was also educational. For example, Florence knew a lot about psychology, and she made me start thinking that my childhood wasn't as happy as I thought it was.

I told her about the time my brother Dave let me roll down the hill in Yonkers, and my infant's fear of falling.

"Not only fear of falling," she said, "but fear of failing."

I'd only begun to think over *that* bombshell when she said, "By the way, when did you start talking?"

I said, "Funny you should ask that. I was a late talker. Not until I was four years old."

"Why did it take you so long?"

"I couldn't commit myself to talk because I didn't think I'd be good at it."

"Aha," she said, "fear of failing."

I got defensive. "But I was writing before I was four."

"Writing when you couldn't talk?"

"No, but I'd sit at a table in the summer parlor for hours with a pad and pencil and make marks that *looked* exactly like writing. Everybody thought it was very cute. It was like the beginning of the foreign-language double-talk I later did at the luncheonette."

Florence asked, "But why did you do it for so many hours at a time?"

Again I hesitated. Then I said, "Because it was a way of getting away from all those giants who could pick me up with one hand."

"Aha," said Florence, "again with a fear."

I was a little annoyed by now, even though what she was saying made sense. "OK, Miss Psychology, explain me this one. When I was about four, my father came home with a Chinese phonograph record. God knows where he got it, probably from some Chinaman who left it behind at the luncheonette or in one of the rooms. We had an old Victrola, the kind you wound up with a crank. I couldn't reach the record, but I could reach the crank. I was home alone a lot and found that I could relieve the tension by cranking up the Victrola and playing that Chinese record with its weird sounds, over and over again. While I listened, I kept walking around and around the border of the rug in the living room.

"Now what is your interpretation of *that?*" I asked triumphantly.

"That one I *can't* figure out," she said. "Let's dance."

So we danced and I thought I finally had won one. But in the middle of "Stardust," Florence whispered in my ear, "That Chinese record held your attention because it was so far removed from your real life, and it probably was some sort of defense against your being alone so much."

That's the way it went all that wonderful summer—talking, philosophizing in the half-assed way that nineteen-year-olds philosophize, looking at the Catskill moon, and dancing.

There was lots of dancing. In previous years I couldn't do much because I had to play in the band. Now I could dance with Florence until one of the Arkins came up to me, snarling, "Don't dance with *her* so much. Dance with one of the ugly girls." All employees of the hotel, from busboy to social director, had to obey this rule of the Catskill resorts. The ugly girls had to be danced with; otherwise, God forbid, they might not come back next season.

On the stage, my work never was better. In the sketches, in the Wednesday night plays produced by Appel, I was doubly motivated. I not only wanted to please Florence, but there was her whole damned family looking at me as if to say, "OK, if you're so talented, let's see you make us laugh."

So I outdid myself to make them laugh—right up through Labor Day, when the summer romance was supposed to come to an end.

But it didn't.

When we got back to New York, we kept seeing each other two or three times a week, until October, when I had to report to the Coast Guard for boot training. I didn't work. I went home to Yonkers, where I "gave to the house" from the two hundred dollars I had earned at the Avon Lodge and kept enough for carfare, movies, and museums for my dates with Florence.

One day I screwed up my courage to ask her what her parents thought about our continuing to date.

She said, "My father summed it up with two syllables: 'Oy vay.' "

# 6
# The Coast Guard Blues

Late in October I had one of my regular dates with Florence. We saw a French movie at the Astor Theater and went for a soda at Schrafft's afterward. It was a wonderful evening. By now, having heard nothing from the Coast Guard, I was beginning to think they had forgotten all about me. Those things happen. I knew one guy in Yonkers whose name got lost in the Selective Service System and who was still working for Otis Elevator a year and a half after his number came up in General Hershey's fishbowl.

That night, when I got home, there was an official U.S. government letter waiting for me. It didn't say "Dear Sir" or "Dear Enlistee" or anything nice. Just "You will report to

Third Coast Guard District, Chambers Street, at 0600 hours, 9 November 1942."

At 0300 (three o'clock in the morning) on 9 November 1942, I got up, packed a small suitcase, and listened to my *Concertino da camera* record for the last time. My mother made me a good breakfast, and it was still early enough for me to say good-bye to everyone in the family. I expected my mother to carry on a lot, but she was quite calm.

I walked over to Kenny Square to get the trolley car. That would take me to the end of the New York City subway, which would then take me to Chambers Street. As I stepped onto the trolley, I said to myself, "This is it, that's all." It was a strange, strange feeling. I thought I'd never be back.

If anyone had told me at that moment that the step onto the trolley car was my first step into a big show business career, I would have said, "You belong in the psycho ward at Bellevue Hospital."

Anyway, I got to Coast Guard headquarters on Chambers Street with plenty of time before 6:00 A.M. There were a lot of nervous guys waiting there. They had shown up even earlier than I did. At 0600, exactly, a chief petty officer came out and yelled, "Every one of you guys with a last name *A* to *L*, on this side of the room. Everybody from *M* to *Z* on that side of the room." When we finished shuffling around, he yelled, "All right. Now all you guys on this side of the room, get on the truck. All you guys on the other side of the room, you go to Manhattan Beach." My group was the Manhattan Beach side. I said to myself, "That's ridiculous. Manhattan Beach is practically down the street, across Brooklyn and near Coney Island. It's right on Sheepshead Bay where Florence and I go for seafood." But I didn't argue. They want to give me Manhattan Beach, I'll take Manhattan Beach.

I won't bore you with the hardships of my boot training at Manhattan Beach. It was no worse than the basic training everyone else had to go through in the military, maybe even less so. The only thing that made it hard for me was the food. I guess I was so spoiled by my mother, Mrs. Fuchs, and the Catskill hotels over the years that I just couldn't get used to the slop that had to be prepared for the fifteen thousand men on the training base. I didn't eat anything but cheese. The rest of the food was deep fried in huge tanks or covered with a gooey white sauce. This is nothing new to anyone who's ever been in the armed forces, but oy, the powdered scrambled eggs and the creamed chipped beef and the greasy cold cuts on Sunday. Other guys got used to it, but I couldn't. I suffered in silence and lost fifty pounds in a month. What with the exercise and close-order drill—plus little or no food—my weight dropped from 220 to 170 pounds.

And my own brother Abe was a cook at Manhattan Beach, too.

I'd go down the chow line and I'd come to Abe behind one of the steam tables, wearing his white apron and chef's cap. I knew that the Coast Guard cooks ate pretty good, so I'd hold out my "slop plate" to Abe, like Oliver Twist, and I'd say, "For God's sake, Abe, I'm your own flesh and blood. Couldn't you slip me a decent piece of meat?"

Abe would say, "We don't play favorites here. You gotta get used to it." He'd dump some powdered mashed potatoes on my plate with slimy brown gravy and say to the next guy, "OK, Mac, what's *your* complaint?"

Anyway, fifty pounds lighter and all, I managed to get through boot training—just like everyone else.

The next crisis came when we finished boot training the day after Christmas and were ready to be shipped out. Once again, Abe could have helped me, but he didn't. No telephone calls were allowed from our part of the base, and I was very upset about not being able to tell Florence where I was going—which could have been anywhere from Australia to Greenland. I said to Abe, who by now was a first-class cook, "You know the other petty officers. Would you please find out where I'm being shipped and let Florence know?" Abe just looked down at me from his six-foot-four-inch frame and pointed to a sign that read: "Loose Lips Sink Ships."

I went back to my barracks and packed my seabag, like all the other guys were doing. The seabags were taken away. "OK, this is it," I said to myself again. We were ordered to fall in outside. We lined up and were marched all the way to the other side of the big base. We turned a corner. There was a main gate, facing out over Sheepshead Bay. There also were two sets of vehicles in the street. On one side there were big trailer trucks. On the other side there was a column of troop carriers. The guy next to me was good at knowing what such things meant. He groaned.

"Why are you groaning?" I asked.

"Because the trailer trucks are where they load your seabags aboard when you are being sent to some other Coast Guard base far away in the United States."

"And the troop carriers?"

"That means you are assigned directly to a ship."

He groaned again. I didn't see the difference.

A chief petty officer came out yelling for us to come to attention. The chiefs were always yelling. He yelled again, "Well, boys, I hope you packed your whites on top of your seabags." (Whites were our white uniforms.) "Because," he continued, "you're going to Gowan' Canal." The way he pronounced it, we all heard it as "Guadalcanal." I had visions

46

of "throw him under the Jeep to get the Jeep out of the sand." I looked at the chief and I thought to myself, "Why is he so happy? He must be sadistic." Now everybody was groaning, not just my buddy.

The chief yelled again. "What the fuck is the matter with you guys? I guess you didn't hear what I said. You're going to *Gowanus* Canal. Pier One. Right here in Brooklyn."

You never saw such happy men. My buddy, who knew about such things, said to me, "Could you fuckin' well believe it? We spend the rest of the fuckin' war guardin' a fuckin' pier, right here in fuckin' Brooklyn."

So we were trucked over to the Gowanus Canal, where we found out that the official name of the station was the Brooklyn Barracks. It was what they called a "COTP Base," COTP meaning captain of the port. It was a pier from which all kinds of war matériel were being shipped overseas. Our job was to make sure that no one stole the airplanes and tanks. We patrolled the pier, five watches a day, with each man doing six hours on and twelve hours off. Every few days you got twenty-four hours off, but you were on the pier every day. Your liberty started at 11:00 P.M. of the day you were on guard, and ended at 11:00 P.M. the next day.

Our job was to patrol a certain section of the pier, carrying a side arm, a pistol, and check off the matériel against a list. But what are you going to do after you check out the pier, stand there and look at the stuff? So we developed a lot of tricks. In cold weather, for example, we'd go in and sit down with the customs people in their nice warm offices and listen to the radio. We'd tip each other off by phone when our chief was coming by on his rounds to make sure we were guarding, not goofing off. Part of the game was to leave your coat outside while you were in with the customs officers. When you heard the chief was coming, you'd pinch your cheeks to make them rosy, then go outside and put on your coat. The chief always checked the buttons to make sure they were cold. While he was feeling the buttons, we'd stamp our feet, blow on our hands and say, "It sure is a cold night, isn't it, Chief?"

Compared with what other men were doing in the service, I can't say we suffered any great hardship. But we *were* bored. The officers knew that, and when another guy and I got the idea of organizing a band for dances on Friday nights, they welcomed the idea.

The other guy was Vernon Duke, the Broadway and classical composer. He was a little fellow and was so nearsighted that he was a total disaster in close-order drill because he couldn't see where he was going. I used to tell him, "Just hold on to my collar," and he'd do that and get through the drills without fucking up. He got promoted to coxswain (the equivalent of sergeant) because, apart from not being able to see, he was very smart. I once asked him how he even passed the physical. He said, "I was so patriotic that I tried every branch of the service. I insisted on serving *somewhere*. They finally figured I could do the least amount of damage in the Coast Guard, so here I am."

Anyway, when we got the notion of forming a band, we went to the base commander, Lieutenant Silverman, who said, "That's a good idea, but it'll have to be unofficial. There's nothing in the Tables of Organization for a dance band. On the other hand, you'll be doing me a favor. If we have dances and let girls on the base just for the evening, maybe the enlisted men will have some incentive to wash and clean themselves up. Right now, they stink."

Duke said, "Yes, sir, I personally guarantee clean seamen at the dances." And the deed was done.

We rounded up every professional musician on the base. Unfortunately, they were all saxophone players, but remembering Shep Fields, I didn't let that stop us. I simply wrote to Shep and asked him for some orchestrations from the days when he had nine saxophones in *his* band. Duke redid the orchestrations and kept changing them as we gradually added a bass player and a drummer. Vernon played the piano himself.

Because we were unofficial, all of us—except Coxswain Duke—had to continue with our seamen's duties. However, Lieutenant Silverman arranged our schedules so that our watches in guarding the pier coincided and we all were free to rehearse at the same time every afternoon. Later, Lieutenant Silverman put us musicians on a construction gang, which was expanding the barracks to accommodate fifteen hundred men. No more guard duty. We worked only in the daytime, hauling lumber and mixing cement. It was much harder work, but much more satisfying. Especially when Lieutenant Silverman told us he wouldn't mind if we used leftover building materials to construct a recreation hall for our dances. When the rec hall and the new barracks were finished, we were moved onto a maintenance detail, correcting all the things we had screwed up while we were in construction. After all, what does a saxophone player know about plumbing fittings?

The Friday night dances were a huge success. Local Brooklyn girls were trucked in—practically in armored cars. Their morals were protected by shore patrols, which ringed the rec hall to make sure the girls didn't disappear anywhere else on the base with the guys. After a while, we were allowed to invite dates. That gave me a chance to see Florence every week. I no longer had to battle time to be with her in New York on those crazy 11:00 P.M. to 11:00 P.M. twenty-four-hour passes.

On the whole, the dances did so much to raise the men's morale (and induce them to wash) that the next step was almost like an old Mickey Rooney-Judy Garland movie, where the kids say, "My uncle has a barn. Let's do a show." There was a lieutenant commander on the base, our medical officer, who had been in amateur theatricals when he was in college and medical school, and that's exactly what he said to Lieutenant Silverman: "Let's do a show—to go along with the dances." The doctor said he could write satirical songs about life on the base. Lieutenant Silverman said, "Work it out with Caesar and Duke."

And so it came about that the three of us—Vernon, the doctor, and I—produced a revue with music called *Six On, Twelve Off*, based on the inflexible Coast Guard patrol schedule for guarding a pier.

Now I *really* was busy. I continued with the maintenance detail, but in my spare time I also had to write sketches and even music (the doctor's material wasn't that good). When we started doing the show every week in the rec hall, I played the saxophone, led the band, and was the chief comic in all the sketches. As the old saying goes, if they'd shoved a broom up my ass, I also could have swept the floor.

The way it ended up, I operated the same as I had done in the Catskills. Someone would come up with an idea about something we could satirize on the base and we would improvise a skit, polishing it until it was as funny as possible. Most of it was inside Coast Guard stuff that wouldn't have gotten any laughs from a general audience. But, being one of the three guys in charge, I could also create some original material that had nothing to do with the Brooklyn Barracks.

For example, I perfected a routine I had fooled around with in the Catskills called "A Conversation between Adolph

Hitler and Donald Duck." I played both parts. I'd be Hitler, yelling and screaming in the German double-talk I'd been doing since I was a kid. Then I'd be Donald Duck, trying to reason with Hitler in his quack-quack voice but also speaking my German double-talk, with an occasional English phrase sneaking in, like, "Aw, why don't you sit down, you crazy bastard."

This routine broke everyone up, especially Vernon Duke. The first time he heard it, he was supposed to follow me with a song he had just written for a Broadway show. It was one of his greatest, "Taking a Chance on Love." But Vernon was laughing so hard, he couldn't get started with the song. The song became a classic; the sketch was forgotten; but that's the way it was in those days.

In *Six On, Twelve Off,* I also began to experiment with the very beginnings of some material that, fortunately, evolved into later stuff that did *not* become forgotten. I was fascinated with aviation movies, always had been since I was a little boy going to RKO Proctors in Yonkers. In the Brooklyn Barracks show, I did two numbers: "The Peacetime Airplane Movie" and "The Wartime Airplane Movie." I played all the parts and did all the sound effects with my mouth.

The peacetime movie was about a test pilot who wouldn't go up in his plane unless his mechanic stuck his wad of chewing gum at the back of the cockpit. Without the gum, the pilot knew he wasn't going to come back. One day the gum flies off. The plane goes into a power dive. The principal character then becomes the altimeter, which I also played along with all the other parts. As the altimeter, I indicated the descent of the plane with my arms swinging—while I did all the other effects of the pilot screaming and vomiting, the engine catching and sputtering, the sound of the wind in the struts, and so on.

Where Have I Been?

The wartime movie was a satire of *Wings, Dawn Patrol*, and all the other World War I aviation epics. "I can't send those kids up in those crates; they have no guns on them. Besides, those kids haven't learned how to fly yet." I did all the sounds of aerial dogfights, the winner saluting the loser as he goes down in flames. And then the sound of the squadron returning to base. The last one sputters coming in, and I make the sound of a big crash. The squadron commander says, happily, "Well, he made it."

As crude as this material was, compared to what I evolved it into later, it was a big hit with the Coast Guard audience. So was the music and the in-joke stuff about guys shooting off their toes or conning the chiefs while they are on watch. Soon, other Coast Guard and Navy officers came to see the show and they asked Lieutenant Silverman if they could borrow us for performances of *Six On, Twelve Off* at their bases. He was very pleased and said, "As long as we get them back." So we spent a lot of time traveling all around the Third Naval District and the Third Coast Guard District with our show.

That was great for me. I was away from the Brooklyn Barracks most weekends now, and I could sneak off and see Florence in Manhattan between shows without the formality of asking for liberty. I was able to be with her when she graduated from Hunter College in June 1943. A couple of weeks later we went to the wedding of some friends of ours. It was all so beautiful that I whispered to Florence after the ceremony, "Why don't *we* get married, too."

She looked up at me with those gorgeous eyes and said, "Why not?"

So on July 17, 1943, a little more than a year after we had first met, Florence and I became man and wife. It was a typical, spare wartime wedding in the Moskowitz and Lupowitz restaurant on the Lower East Side in Manhattan. Florence's parents were there and didn't look too happy. My parents were there and made it very clear they thought I was crazy because both the bride and groom were only twenty years old. My mother said, "What's the hurry? But if it makes you happy . . ." Neither set of parents had much to say to the other.

My best man was Coxswain Vernon Duke—just about to be *ex*-Coxswain Vernon Duke. He and the Coast Guard had decided that for the good of the service, it might be best for them to part ways. He was returning to the civilian theater to write another musical comedy.

I was kind of sad when that nice little guy clapped me on the shoulder after the ceremony was over and wished me and Florence all the best. He may have been the one person in the room who meant it without qualification. Then he said, "Who knows? Maybe we'll work together again soon, buddy."

I said, gloomily, "Yeah, who knows?" I thought he was crazy.

But we all got into the spirit of the event with a nice wedding reception. I played the saxophone and Vernon played the piano.

Then Florence and I went off to a one-night honeymoon at the Hotel Manhattan (I had to be back at the base at 2100 hours the next night)—and Vernon Duke wandered off into civilian life forever.

Or so I thought.

# 7

## *Tars and Spars:* A Commodore Kept Me Out of the Brig

I really missed Vernon. The dances and shows at the base didn't seem the same without him.

But I did get to see him occasionally in his civilian life. He was such a nice guy and a good friend. He knew how hungry I always was on Coast Guard food, so he used to invite me to his apartment on East Thirty-fifth Street in New York for a decent meal whenever I got a liberty to spend with my new wife, Florence. "You should never see Florence on an empty stomach," he said. "Besides, knowing your appetite, you'd blow your whole thirty-dollar-a-month pay in the first restaurant you passed with her."

So, on my way to Florence's house (she was still living with her parents, of course), I'd drop in at Vernon's for a fortifying meal. With his involvement in the upper levels of the music world, I never knew what to expect when I got there.

I'll never forget the time I arrived, starved, and found Vernon in an earnest conversation with Gregor Piatigorsky, the great concert cellist. With my stomach rumbling, I sat patiently, listening to them discuss the ending of a movement of a concerto they were writing. They were both speaking Russian. I'd hear Vernon say a few words in Russian and then mouth some musical notes: "Bup-bup-de-bup-bup-bup-de-bup-bup." Then Piatigorsky would say, *"Nyet, nyet.* Bup-bup-bup-de-bup-de-bup-de-bup-bup-bup."

It went back and forth like that, and finally I was so hungry I couldn't stand it anymore. I walked over to the table where they were sitting and I spouted a long speech in my double-talk Russian, followed by *my* version of how the concerto movement should end: "Bup-bup-bup-de-bup-bup-bup-de-bup-bup." Piatigorsky said, *"Da,"* Vernon said, "That solves it," and we all went to the dining room to eat. Not that they even remotely accepted my version, but they both were hungry by then, too, and my intervention presented them with a nice way of getting out of their impasse—for the time being—without either of them losing face.

It was exciting—and so were the subsequent hours I spent with Florence. I couldn't wait until the damned war was over and we could have our own place together. Everything was so marvelous when we were alone, but I began to hate hotel rooms.

Then a lot of strange things began to happen in quick succession.

One day Vernon just disappeared, leaving no forwarding address.

About a week later, Lieutenant Silverman, the base commander, called me into his office. He had a set of military orders from Washington in his hand. He was rubbing his chin, obviously puzzled. He said, "When I get a set of orders saying Vice-Admiral So-and-so should report to another base, that I can understand. When I get a set of orders saying that a thousand seamen should report to another base, that, too, I can understand. But when I get this set of orders saying that just one Seaman First Class, Sidney Caesar, Serial Number 646717, should report to Coast Guard Barracks, Biltmore Hotel, Palm Beach, Florida—*that* I *don't* understand."

I didn't understand it either, but I saluted and took the orders from Lieutenant Silverman, who said, "Whatever it is, I wish you luck."

Attached to the orders was a travel warrant for a train to Florida, leaving that night. I barely had time to meet Florence for a quick good-bye. It wasn't until I boarded the train, jam-packed with civilians and soldiers and sailors going on leave, that it occurred to me that I had never before been farther south than Asbury Park, New Jersey.

I guess all wartime travel was miserable in those days, but this train trip was particularly miserable, with frequent stops on sidings to let military freight go by. I was groggy when I finally arrived at the super-fancy Palm Beach Biltmore, which had been converted into a Coast Guard station.

But what *kind* of Coast Guard station?

I found out when a familiar figure walked up to me in the lobby. It was Vernon Duke. I couldn't believe it, but he was wearing the uniform of a full lieutenant in the Coast Guard. "Hi, Sid," he said, "I guess you're wondering why I asked you here." I was so startled I didn't even follow through on his question. I said, "What's with the officer's uniform? You're a civilian."

He said, "Not anymore, I'm not. They called me back into the Coast Guard and made me a lieutenant. You remember how someone in the Brooklyn Barracks once said, 'Let's do a show,' and we did it?"

I said vaguely, "Yeah, I remember."

He said, "Well, that's what's happened here on a big scale. Coast Guard headquarters in Washington called me in and said, 'The army has a show, *This Is the Army*, the air corps is working on a show, so why shouldn't the Coast Guard have a show? The civilians see it, and it's good for recruiting.' So they made me a lieutenant and here I am. Howard Dietz and I are writing the show. We have a working title, *Tars and Spars*. So why don't you ask me what *you* are doing here?"

"OK, I'll ask. What am I doing here?"

"I requested you—as a chorus boy. The billing on the show will be Victor Mature, Gower Champion, and Fifty Others. The others are forty-nine other guys and you. What I really wanted you for is that crazy airplane-movie routine you did up in Brooklyn. I want to build that up into a full-scale number for you."

I could hardly believe it. "Could I get some chow and some sleep first?" I said.

That was the beginning of an experience that seemed like the Land of Oz to me. One day I'm fixing toilets at the Brooklyn Barracks; two days later I'm in a room at the Palm

Beach Biltmore and rehearsing all day in the Grand Ballroom with a big movie star like Victor Mature and a great choreographer like Gower Champion, both Coast Guardsmen. It all was so unreal that I didn't even dream about being the Number One Comic. That spot was reserved for another Coast Guardsman named Marc Bolero, who had a lot of professional experience as an impressionist in vaudeville. After all, I was just the rankest of amateurs.

For a few days I learned some dance steps from Gower, with the rest of the chorus, and Vernon worked me into a sketch or two. Then, a little fellow with bright brown eyes and wispy hair showed up. He was introduced to the cast as Max Liebman, who was to be the civilian director of the show. It was explained that he was a little late because he had just finished a movie with Danny Kaye in Hollywood.

I knew all about Max Liebman. To those of us who had worked in the Catskills, Max was the Great Ziegfeld of the Borscht Circuit. For fifteen years, he had been the producer of summer shows at the Tamiment resort in the Poconos in Pennsylvania. Danny Kaye was only one of the big stars he had developed at Tamiment. One of Max's Tamiment shows, *Straw Hat Revue*, even had made it to Broadway. He was known as a genius.

So I was amazed when he came to me soon after he arrived and said, "Now, Caesar, about that airplane-movie number of yours. Do it for me."

I nervously did it—both the peacetime version and the wartime version.

Liebman said, "Very amateurish, but you've got a good idea there. Now, here's what we're going to do. We're going to drop the peacetime movie and stick to the wartime movie alone. We're going to do it as an out-and-out parody of *Wings*.

58

We're going to do a whole plot about an American ace who is always smiling, and a German ace who is always snarling. We are going to have them in typical Hollywood World War I dogfights, and of course we will have the smiling American win."

I interrupted. "Excuse me, Mr. Liebman, but you keep saying 'we.' Who is 'we'?"

"We," he said, "is you and I. We are going to write this number together."

I, a little *schlepper*, writing with Max Liebman? I couldn't believe it.

Max and I, working on it every day, gradually refined the airplane number into a fully fleshed-out, nine-minute monologue. Only it wasn't really a monologue. With all the characters I played, plus all the sound effects I mouthed, it began to seem like there was a whole stageful of people and props— not just me. After a while, even the stagehands laughed in rehearsals, and it's not easy to make stagehands laugh.

One day, just before we were ready to open, Vernon Duke said to me, "Nice job on the war-movie routine. Now, do you remember that other thing you did in Brooklyn that broke me up—the conversation between Hitler and Donald Duck?"

I said, "Sure."

He said, "We need a quick filler, so we're going to put that one in the show, too. You won't need Max Liebman's help this time. Just give us a minute and a half of that crazy kraut double-talk of yours. I'm laughing again just thinking about it."

So when *Tars and Spars* opened in Palm Beach, I had two solo numbers and parts in about six of the sketches. And when I was needed to play the saxophone, I played the saxophone. It was a very exhausting night. The reviews were good, with Vic Mature and Gower Champion receiving most of the attention, as was to be expected. But to remind us that we still were Coast Guardsmen, our chief had us all out doing close-order drill the very next day.

We played a week in Palm Beach, then moved to Jacksonville for a week. By now it was apparent what lay ahead of us. Word leaked out that we were being financed by Columbia Pictures, which held an option for a possible future movie version of *Tars and Spars*. Therefore, unlike *This Is the Army*, which played in legitimate theaters for several weeks at a time, we had a succession of one-week bookings in movie houses, all of which still had vaudeville stages in those days. It was a grind, six shows a day from early in the morning to late at night, usually with a Columbia movie on the screen between performances. There hardly was time for close-order drill to remind us how lucky we were not to be on a ship somewhere, being shot at by the Germans or Japanese.

We went to Atlanta, Baltimore, and all the way up the East Coast. My solo numbers got bigger and bigger applause as we went along. Although my name wasn't billboarded outside, I was becoming one of the stars of the show. By this time Vernon Duke and Max Liebman were gone, having finished their job of whipping the production into shape. Our commanding officer now was a strict do-it-by-the-book Coast Guarder named Lieutenant Cook, who gave me and everyone else a rough time. He never let us forget for a minute we were just seamen on detached duty, which could be *temporary* duty with any infraction of the rules. Somehow it all was tougher on me than the others. I had become very, very nervous and distraught, not being able to be with Florence.

Thinking back, I realize now that perhaps everything came too easily for me in those early days—and even later. I never really was prepared for any adversity. I'd always had a protector, someone who believed in my talent and looked after me. First, there was Don Appel and then Vernon Duke. Even in those bad times when *Tars and Spars* was moving up the coast, I had an unseen protector I didn't even know about at the time. He was Commodore (later Admiral) Reed Hill, in Coast Guard headquarters in Washington. He apparently had followed my career since my days at the Brooklyn Barracks. I suspect it was Vernon Duke who acquainted him with both my potential and my weaknesses. Commodore Hill had issued my orders to report to Palm Beach for *Tars and Spars,* and it was Commodore Hill who made sure I would continue with the show so that I could still be available if the Columbia Pictures movie ever materialized. Commodore Hill was at the side of Coast Guard Commandant Admiral Wachie, who came to our performance in Philadelphia to announce to us that a deal for the eventual film *had* been made.

Most important, it was Commodore Hill who saved my ass and literally kept me from spending the rest of the war in the brig.

I was building up to my first mental breakdown. It happened finally when *Tars and Spars* reached Buffalo, New York. It was our sixth week on the road and I was getting kind of crazy. I blamed the fact that the war-movie number I did was taking so much out of me—but the causes ran deeper than that. When we opened in the Buffalo movie theater, the name of which I don't even remember, the first show was at 9:00 A.M. I walked out on the stage to do my war-movie number and I couldn't see more than about a dozen people in the audience. Two guys were walking around with a naked light bulb on the end of a wire, cleaning up. The others were talking or sleeping. The war-movie number ordinarily took nine minutes. I did a compact version of the routine in four minutes.

When I came offstage, our commanding officer, Lieutenant Cook, was standing there. His face was all red. He screamed, "You go right back out there and do that number right."

I said, "But. . . ."

He said, "And that's an order."

I said, "But . . ."

He said, "I hope you heard me. That's an *order*."

I don't know what came over me, but I picked up a fire bucket filled with sand—weighing about fifty pounds—and I threw it at the lieutenant. I've always been pretty strong, and that fifty-pound missile sailed through the air for about twelve feet and just missed his head.

Suddenly a bunch of guys were grabbing me and holding me down, and then carrying me out to a Jeep. I heard someone say, "Take him to the hospital."

The next thing I knew I was at the U.S. Marine Corps Hospital in Buffalo.

They gave me a shot to calm me down, and in the morning I had a session with a navy psychiatrist. He asked me, "Why did you do it?"

I explained how there were only about fifteen people in the audience and I couldn't perform all out. I tried to describe the tensions of building up to do a complicated routine like the war-movie number six times a day.

The doctor looked at me as if I were crazy—no pun intended. He shook his head and said, "I can understand what happens with incoming mortar rounds, 155-millimeter howitzers, and thousand-pound bombs. But not doing the airplane number in a show, I *can't* understand." I was sent back to my ward.

Lying in bed the next morning, I heard two marines come in. They were talking loudly. I couldn't tell whether they were patients or hospital personnel. But I could hear them loud and clear. All they were talking about was Jews, Hebes, kikes, sheenies—and how yellow they were. I never had run into much anti-Semitism before, and I figured these guys would soon switch their attacks to micks, wops, niggers, spicks, Polacks, and hunkies—which is what used to happen with such outbursts in Yonkers. But all they kept talking about was "yellow Jews."

I had to get up to take a leak. Out of the corner of my eye, I saw these two guys walk over to my bed and check my chart. The chart lists religion, in case they have to call in a chaplain. When I got back from the bathroom, I heard one of them say to the other, "I *told* you this one was a yellow Jew."

Very calmly, I thought, I walked over to my bed and picked up my glass water pitcher. I smashed it on the edge of the bedstand. Then I grabbed one of the marines—the other one ran away—and I pressed the jagged edge of the broken pitcher against his neck. I said, "Now, how yellow are these Jews?"

The other marine was screaming for the orderlies. A bunch of them came running in. They grabbed me and rushed me downstairs to the same psychiatrist who had first interviewed me.

The doctor said, "What is *this?*"

I said, "A guy keeps calling you kike, yellow, all sorts of other nasty things, it kind of gets on your nerves."

"Were you going to kill him?"

"I don't know if I would have killed him. I would have cut him."

Strangely, the psychiatrist seemed kind of relieved. He said, "Not doing the airplane number in the show I can't understand. *This* I can understand."

And that was it.

They kept me in the hospital for ten days. Then I got a set of orders sending me home for another ten days of sick leave. The orders were from Commodore Reed Hill's office in Washington.

I went back to Yonkers, and Florence joined me at my parents' house. I never was so glad to see anyone in my life. Her quiet strength, her understanding, was all I needed to pull myself together again.

Just before the ten days were up, another set of orders came from the commodore. I don't remember the exact wording, but the official orders said, in effect, "Seaman First Class Sidney Caesar will rejoin the *Tars and Spars* production in Kansas City. Mrs. Sidney Caesar will accompany Seaman Caesar to Kansas City and will remain with him throughout the remainder of the production's tour. This action is unusual, but it is for the good of the service."

# 8

## *Tars and Spars,* Hollywood: Who's the Blond Kid?

For the good of the *service?* Now you know what I mean when I say that I was too coddled, too spoiled, that it all was too easy for me in those days; that I even had gotten away with attempted murder in Buffalo; that one of the seeds of my future problems was being planted. Show business hype had invaded the armed forces and show business investments had to be protected. I occasionally feel guilty at the special treatment I received—even being allowed to have my wife with me on wartime active duty. But at the time, of course, I thought it was great.

I received a ten-dollars-a-day allowance on which Florence and I could live quite comfortably in separate quarters while we were on the road. I don't know if the other guys in the show resented it. Nobody ever said anything to me, and it's possible that Vic Mature and others had the same arrangement. Maybe it wasn't even too unusual. I later learned that the army gave similar "quarters and rations allowances" to the editors and reporters of *Yank* magazine, all of whom were enlisted men and lived where they pleased.

With me, the presence of Florence was a complete tonic. She loved me, calmed me down, kept my temper in check. All my anxieties disappeared and my performances improved. She's a strong woman—even then, when she was only twenty-two—and her just being there was enough to make the rest of the tour a joy.

We went from Kansas City, on through the midwestern and mountain states, and finally to the West Coast. Our last performances were in Los Angeles and we stayed on to begin production of the movie. When Columbia Pictures took over, a lot of strange things happened. Victor Mature was out and a civilian, Alfred Drake, was brought in as the star of *Tars and Spars.* A love story was added, between Drake and Janet Blair. As the comic in the show-within-a-show, I became the third lead, as Alfred Drake's pal. In those days in the movies, the comic *always* was the leading man's pal.

As the production dragged on, delayed by a movie industry strike, Florence and I lived in a furnished room that cost forty dollars a month. That seemed like Fat City to us on my sixty-six-dollars-a-month Coast Guard pay and the ten-dollars-a-day allowance. Even when I wasn't working, I'd go to the studio every day to try to find out what Hollywood was all about. I found out some interesting things. The new choreographer, for example, was Jack Cole, assisted by Gwen Verdon. One Monday morning Cole showed up with his entire body shaved. "Why did you do that?" I asked. "I had nothing else to do," he said. "Oh," I said.

With our Coast Guard personnel, discipline was breaking down. Once in a while they'd take us outside and march us down the street, and that was just about our only remaining connection with military life. It was August 1945, the war was over, and people were getting discharged. I stayed on a little longer because one of the last scenes to be filmed was my airplane-movie number. The director, Alfred Greene, asked me how long it would take and I said, "Exactly nine minutes after you set up your cameras." He thought I was nuts, but I had so fine-tuned the routine by then that it didn't take much more time than that.

We no longer had a commanding officer. Instead, there was Coast Guard Lieutenant Commander Milton Bren, who was our "liaison" with the studio and had an office there. He was a nice man, who introduced me to people like Pandro Berman, the producer, and songwriters Sammy Cahn and Jule Styne. Bren was a real estate man in civilian life, but he had a lot of contacts in the movie business.

One day, as the picture was finishing up, Bren said to me, "How would you like to make a thousand dollars?"

I said, incredulously, "A *thousand* dollars?"

He said, "That's just the bonus. You'll make five hundred dollars a week."

I was still in a daze. I said, "Five *hundred* dollars a week? *Every* week?"

He said, "No. Forty weeks."

Bren explained that I'd be working for him, that I'd be paid directly by him, and that he'd make deals with movie studios for my services—just as big producers like David O. Selznick used to do in those days.

I signed the papers and took his thousand-dollar check. I went immediately to the bank so I could bring the money to Florence, all in cash. She went right out and rented us a nice furnished apartment for one hundred twenty-five dollars a month, though she was a little skeptical about the deal. Later, Bren and I did have a legal dispute about its validity. My defense was, "I was under orders. I was a seaman first class, you were a lieutenant commander, and you ordered me to sign the contract." That got the dispute settled and the deal did not remain in effect.

In the meantime, though, Bren got me another film with Columbia. It was *The Guilt of Janet Ames*, starring Melvyn Douglas and Rosalind Russell. Before I began work on the picture, there was a sneak preview of *Tars and Spars* in Santa Barbara, about a hundred miles from Los Angeles. Florence and I went to see the movie and we didn't like it very much. The studio had degenerated it into a typical servicemen's epic, like the ones Van Johnson seemed to be doing every other week.

We had no way of getting back to Los Angeles when the preview was over, so we were offered a lift by Morris Stoloff, Columbia's musical director. Stoloff seemed excited. He said, "Do you know anything about preview cards?" I said I didn't and he explained. "That's what the audience fills out when they leave the theater. With this picture, nearly everyone wrote, 'Who's the kid with the blond hair? Let's see more of him.' Do you know what that means, son? I think you're going to be a big, big star."

My mind was totally incapable of grasping that. I couldn't

comprehend what Stoloff was saying. I just felt confused and helpless.

All the way back to Los Angeles, I kept thinking of the time my brother Dave let me roll down the hill in Yonkers and, in my infant mind, there were no hands on the carriage.

# 9

# "If You Take Care, You'll Be All Right"

The war finally over, I was now officially out of the Coast Guard and trying to adjust to becoming a full-time civilian again. It was all kind of unreal. Florence and I were living in that luxurious furnished apartment with nothing of our own but our clothes and a few pots and pans. We couldn't make any plans for some kind of permanency because *Tars and Spars* wouldn't open until January 1946, and only then would I know if I had any future in the movie industry. Stoloff and a few others were enthusiastic about me, but who knew what the overall public would think when the picture went into general release? I didn't put much faith in my arrangement with Milton Bren. If *Tars and Spars* bombed and I went down with the sinking ship, why should he keep me on his personal payroll at five hundred dollars a week?

I began the one film job he had set up for me, *The Guilt of Janet Ames*. I loved working with Melvyn Douglas, one of my idols from my childhood moviegoing days at the RKO Proctors in Yonkers. My part was very small, though, and I didn't get to spend much time with him. I played a stand-up nightclub comic. My one big scene was a dream sequence in which I was the comic doing his act. Watching the filming of the picture every day, I realized what a ridiculous psychological mishmash it was. So, for my dream-sequence comedy act, I made up a satire of a psychiatrist, which really was a satire of the very movie we were making. I didn't think they'd let me get away with it, but they did. Maybe they didn't know what I was up to, or maybe they just thought it was an improvement on the script. Anyway, I had sown the seeds of a successful routine I was to do many versions of in the future—the eccentric psychiatrist.

At home Florence and I were playing house—as best we could in a furnished apartment. We had a lot of laughs, especially when I tried to teach her how to cook, from my experience in my father's luncheonette. After eating a lot of half-raw eggs, I had to let her in on the secret that a three-minute egg means three minutes after the water is *boiling*. But we made joint mistakes, too. Pressure cookers were just coming on the market then, and we bought one. I'll never forget when we tried to cook a steak in the gadget. It came out like a slab of concrete. Then we tried baking it, broiling it, and boiling it. No go. Laughing all the way, we finally went out to the Brown Derby for dinner.

## Where Have I Been?

We were learning to live together and Florence shared my tears as well as my laughter. The studio sent us back to New York for Christmas with the proviso that I do a little publicity for *Tars and Spars* on the side. When I got home, I learned that my father was very ill. He had cancer—something nobody ever talked about at the time—which is why my family had not let me know. Florence explained this to me and kept me from falling apart.

The studio had put us up at the Hotel Pierre. I was sitting there one day trying to figure out what I could do for my father, when I had an idea. I picked up the phone and called Al Rylander, who was publicity director for Columbia Pictures. I said, "Have you scheduled any previews of *Tars and Spars?*"

Rylander said, "Yes, we have. Why do you ask?"

I explained about how ill my father was and that I'd like him to see the picture.

He said, "How far can he travel?"

I said, "Not far."

He said, "OK, then. We'll switch one of the previews from Loew's Delancey downtown to Loew's Paradise in the Bronx. That's pretty close to Yonkers." Al Rylander was a very nice man.

We went to Yonkers on the night of the preview, and we drove my father down to Loew's Paradise. I couldn't take my eyes off him. This symbol of strength in my childhood was now over seventy, thin, wasted, and defeated.

When we got to the theater and *Tars and Spars* began, I still couldn't look at anything but my father. I didn't see a single frame of the film. There was applause after my airplane number, but I didn't turn my gaze from my father, even then. He just kept staring at the screen, saying nothing.

He didn't say anything in the car on the way home either. But finally, in the living room, he spoke.

He said, "You say you make five hundred dollars a week?"

"Yes, Papa," I said.

"Put some away," he said. "If you take care, you'll be all right." It was the only approval of my career he ever had been able to express. But I like to think he also was expressing his feeling that he didn't have to worry about me anymore and that if he had to die, he'd die happy.

As we drove away from the house in Yonkers, he was watching us from the window. I told Florence, "We'll never see him again."

I was right. A few weeks later, there was a call from my brother Dave at six o'clock in the morning, and I had to fly back from Hollywood for the funeral.

Dave told me that at least Papa had seen the reviews of *Tars and Spars*. The picture had been rapped but not me. Wanda Hale wrote in the *New York Daily News*: "Sid Caesar is a real comedy find. His interpretation of an air force movie is alone worth the price of admission." Dave said that Papa had kept that review at his bedside, nearly up to the end.

I sadly flew back to Los Angeles. The real implications of my father's death didn't strike me until later. At that time I was mostly worried about my mother. But I knew she was strong and that Abe and Dave, neither of whom had married, were still living at home with her. Also, I was still "giving to the house."

Back in Hollywood, I began to wonder about how long I could contribute as much as I did. Despite my good reviews in *Tars and Spars*, nothing was happening. Alfred Greene, who had directed that picture, wanted me to play Al Jolson in *The Jolson Story* for Columbia. I said, "That's ridiculous. I can't play Jolson." But Columbia gave me a screen test for the part anyway. Greene looked at it and said to me, "You're right." Larry Parks got the role.

I was mostly playing tennis and swimming. A telephone call would upset my routine. One day I got a call from New York, and that already was an exciting event. It was Monte Proser, who staged the shows at the Copacabana nightclub. I had met him at a party and he had told me how much he liked me in *Tars and Spars*. On the phone he said, "How would you like to do a couple of weeks at the Copa?"

I said, "I have no material."

He said, "You'll get something."

I didn't know what to do. The only person I could think of for advice was Max Liebman, who was making it very big in New York since he had finished helping put *Tars and Spars* together for the stage. Max said, "Why are you hanging around Hollywood? They don't know how to use you out there. Besides, I personally will help you write an act for the Copa."

That settled it. I ended my contractual relationship with Milton Bren, and Florence and I packed up our clothes and pots and pans (and the pressure cooker), and moved back to New York. I sat down to write with Liebman. Starting with the nine-minute airplane-movie number, we added three other numbers to round out a twenty-five-minute act. That's all you had to do at the Copacabana in those days. There always was a singer on the bill, and the Copa Girls chorus line filled out the rest of the time. I opened on New Year's Day of 1947, and nobody booed me or threw anything at me, so I guess I was all right. I was amazed when I picked up the newspapers the next day and saw that the critics said I was a smash.

I finished out the two weeks and Max said, "A good start.

Now I'll take you to my agent, William Morris, and they'll get bookings for you all over the country. I'll go with you. You've got a lot to learn. We want you to be ready for a lot of things that could happen to us in the future."

Again it was "we" and "us." That made me feel good—and comfortable. I had another protector. There were hands on the carriage again.

So we did the nightclub and movie-theater vaudeville circuit, and I soon found out that Max was right. I had a lot to learn—including not letting myself get out of control. For example, there was an incident in Baltimore that was a throwback to the time I threw the sand bucket at Lieutenant Cook in Buffalo, and also a forerunner to some even more serious things to come. And I wasn't even drinking then. But I was on the verge.

I was playing the Club Charles in Baltimore. By now, Max and I had developed my act to a solid forty-five minutes, including a very funny bit about how people express their love in various countries of the world. I did the whole forty-five minutes on opening night and never got a single laugh.

I went to the owner of the club and I said, "I gotta get out of here. I mean, there's nobody laughing, you don't want *me*. What the hell? You don't have to pay me."

He said, "You must be out of your fuckin' mind. Do you realize this is the first time it's been quiet in here? Nobody's talking, nobody's eating. They're paying attention. So you'll just finish the engagement, kid. I will *not* let you out of your contract."

I was steaming mad. I went back to my hotel room and right after I walked in, I grabbed the sink and literally ripped it out of the wall. In my blind rage, I didn't realize at first that the porcelain had shattered and had severed an artery in my hand. When I saw the bright red blood spurting about four inches into the air, I wrapped a towel around the hand and ran next door, to Max's room.

I said, "Max, we're gonna have to go to the hospital."

He said, "What for?"

Unwrapping the towel and letting the blood spurt up again, I said, "For this." He nearly fainted, but he got me to the hospital. He said, "You're too strong to have such a temper, kid. You've got to keep it in check." At the hospital, they stitched up the hand. I still have the scar.

I obviously couldn't take rejection, whether real or imagined, but for the most part, I didn't have to suffer it very much. I continued to do well. The Roxy Theater in New York booked me several times, for example, and kept raising my salary until it reached thirty-five hundred a week.

The Roxy was in Rockefeller Center, and when I played there, I ate most of my meals at Lindy's Restaurant, about a block away. The owner of the restaurant was Leo Lindy, a well-known Broadway character, made famous by writers like Damon Runyon and columnists Walter Winchell and Earl Wilson. Leo became a good friend of mine.

One day Leo came by the Roxy with a man he introduced as "Joe Hyman, the producer." Hyman said, "I was just out front watching your act. I don't like you." Remembering what Max had told me about holding my temper, I said, "OK, so you don't like me. Good-bye."

Hyman said, "Whether I like you or not doesn't matter. Other people like you. I'm putting together a Broadway revue called *Make Mine Manhattan* and I have a spot in it for a comic of your type. How much do you make here at the Roxy?"

I said, "Thirty-five hundred dollars a week."

He said, "I'll pay you two hundred and fifty."

By then, I was getting wise to the ways of show business. I said, "Fine. But no run-of-the-play contract. All I want is that I can give you two weeks notice, just the same as you can give me two weeks notice."

He said OK, but I could see he was confused. He couldn't decide if I was totally insane, or if I had something up my sleeve.

So I went to work for Hyman while I continued to do my act at the Roxy. His show still was in the process of development so I didn't have to be there all the time. The revue was to be a collection of songs and sketches, all about the island of Manhattan. Hyman had signed some good people for the show, among them David Burns and Sheila Bond, and his writers already had come up with some excellent sketch material. In one very funny sketch, Dave Burns, one of the best comics in the country, played a retired old man who refused to evacuate his park bench for a movie company which was filming in that very spot. I was the British director who had to contend with him while he kibbitzed everything the film crew was doing. Dave's character was a man who had been in the clothing business and he spoke with a Yiddish accent. The denouement of the skit came when he criticized the movie's costumes and I got into a violent argument with him. I finally forgot my "veddy veddy British" manner of speech and said, in an accent as Yiddish-tinged as Burns's, "When it comes to a garment, I already forgot what you ever knew."

As time went on, I began to create my own material—aided by Max Liebman—for further sketches in the show. Hyman accepted them. One of my sketches, which I did solo, was about a lowly gumball machine that kept getting beat up when it delivered only the one required gumball for each penny. It decided that honesty was not the best policy and that if it was going to get beat up anyway, it would keep the gum *and* the pennies. The owner of the machine said, "Hey, this kid has talent," and promoted it to be a flashy twenty-five-cent slot machine.

Another of my skits derived—as so much of my material did—from my personal experiences with Florence. A satire on inflation, it showed the difference between a couple going out on a date in 1938, and then again in 1948—ten years later.

I remembered how Florence and I had gone to a place called Rex's on Ninth Avenue, where we had a glass of wine, antipasto, minestrone soup, a small steak with pasta, and spumoni—ninety cents, with a fifteen-cent tip. For $2.10, I was the biggest man. And then we went to a Broadway show, two tickets, $2.20. After that, I had enough money for a soda and a hansom cab ride in Central Park. The total cost of the whole date: $5.00. By contrast, in 1948, the year of *Make Mine Manhattan*, five dollars wouldn't even cover the taxi fare.

So for the show, I did the story of a 1938 date and then a 1948 date, beginning each with the song:

*Hello, Baby, you'd better get ready*
*I'm comin' down to get my steady*
*We'll do the town, and maybe we'll rocket*
*Because I've got five dollars*
*And it's burnin' a hole in my pocket.*

In the 1938 date, I used a French accent for the cocktail lounge waiter and an Italian accent for the restaurant waiter, and so on. The same accents popped up in the same places on the 1948 date, but mostly to kick us out because the five dollars wasn't enough to pay for *anything*. How strange this all seems in retrospect today, when such an evening probably would cost two *hundred* dollars.

Anyway, the routine went into the show—nearly eighteen minutes. Originally, I was supposed to do only two numbers, but by the time we opened in New Haven, I was in twelve of the twenty-one items of the revue. The opening-night notices came out, and we were labeled a big hit by the critics. The second night, it was standing room only, and it continued that way through our run at the Shubert in New Haven. Something unheard of was happening. Joe Hyman, the producer, was making money on the *road*. He must have remembered that he only had me under contract for two weeks because he began to look at me nervously.

We moved to the Forrest Theater in Philadelphia, and Hyman got to be even more nervous. Again the critics raved and again we had SRO audiences. The third night in Philadelphia, Hyman came up to me—all sweetness and smiles— and he said, "Sidney, my boy, we gotta talk."

I said, "So talk."

He said, "About that clause you have in our contract where you have the option to walk out on me with two weeks notice. How can I bring a hit show into New York with a star who can leave whenever he wants?"

I said, "That's a good question."

He said, "Maybe I was a little hasty when I made that deal with you back at the Roxy Theater."

I said, "Maybe you were a little hasty when you only offered me two hundred and fifty dollars a week."

He said, "Have a drink."

I said, "No, we'll have a drink afterward."

He said, "Make me an offer."

I said, "Fifteen hundred dollars a week plus five percent of the box office."

He gulped and said, "Are you sure you don't want a drink?"

I said, "I'm sure."

He then settled for what I wanted.

But it was no accident that Hyman was trying to soften me up with alcohol in this confrontation, which he knew he no longer could avoid. He was aware that I had begun to hit the booze pretty hard after rehearsals, and that if he got me smashed, he might be able to come away with a better deal—since I had no agent.

I've always had a bad cough when I get nervous. I even cough onscreen, which sometimes disconcerts audiences. When I think back to that *Make Mine Manhattan* period, my coughing gets so bad that I can't stop. I'm sure it's because this enormously successful show marked the very beginning of the chemical dependency that eventually nearly destroyed me.

I had never done much drinking before. With my parents, it was only the sip of wine at Passover or in the *shul*. With Florence, we never ordered anything more than a glass of "something sweet," like crème de cacao. In the Coast Guard, I was the only guy in my unit who never went on liberty just to get bombed.

During the rehearsals for *Make Mine Manhattan*, however, I began to drink Scotch in my dressing room when the night's work was over. I don't know why I did it. I didn't like the taste; I never got to like the taste. It was just that after I forced down the first two drinks, I *thought* the whiskey made me feel good. It didn't really. I know now it just anesthetized me temporarily from tensions and fears I didn't want to face.

My father was much on my mind those days. I was still steeped in the old traditions and I felt guilty that I had been making so much money. Was it right for a son to outdo his father?

Also, I had a belated reaction to my father's bankruptcies, his total defeat in life, his death.

Was his fate an ominous forecast of what was in store for me? After all, I didn't even comprehend the mysterious source of my talent and my income, so wasn't it possible that it all could be taken away from me someday?

Booze pushed all those thoughts out of my head.

# 10

# "A Show Is Being Canceled Because It's Bringing In Too Much Business?"

Florence didn't notice at first. I'd come home high, but not really drunk, and she must have attributed it to the excitement of my work in the show.

I didn't see as much of her as I used to because I was at work most of the time and she was busy with other things. Throughout much of 1947, she was pregnant with our first child, Michele, called Shelly; and she kept looking around for places for us to live. At first we had a little four-room furnished apartment on West Sixty-sixth Street. It was grandly called the Penthouse, but it really was a converted pigeon coop perched up there all by itself on the roof. The building's elevator didn't even go up that far. That's how the postwar apartment situation was in New York.

Next, we moved to another four-room apartment on West Fifty-eighth Street. It had been furnished and decorated by a landlord of the nonheterosexual persuasion. I still remember the cupid embossed into the wall over the bed.

Finally, when Shelly was born, Florence put her foot down and made it very clear that it was time we had an apartment and furniture of our own—even if we had to move out of crowded Manhattan. So we found a nice four-and-a-half-room apartment in Rego Park in Queens, and that's where Shelly began to grow up.

Shelly was a constant wonder to me. Having been raised in a family of boys only, and not having any nieces, I didn't know how to handle the idea of having a little girl around the house. At one point, Florence said to me, "For God's sake, stop treating her like a doll you bought me from F.A.O. Schwarz. She's a real-life human *person*." But I kept making the same mistake my father made with me. I was too busy, and on my one day off a week, I was too tired.

Only Florence's hands were on Shelly's carriage.

From the time it opened on Broadway, *Make Mine Manhattan* was a solid hit and I remained with the show for a full year. At the end of that time, I was flattered when I was replaced by the great comedian Bert Lahr.

I left because I figured one year was enough. I had ac-cumulated a lot of money and Florence and I both deserved a rest, so we went up to her uncle's Avon Lodge in the Catskills. When I returned, there was a message from Max Liebman, who was back at Tamiment in the Poconos, doing his shows. I phoned Max and he said he wanted to come into New York to have lunch with me and Pat Weaver.

I said, "Who's Pat Weaver?"

He said, "He's a vice-president of NBC in charge of television."

Remember, this was 1949. I said, "You mean television is already so important, it has a vice-president of its own at NBC?"

Max said, "Just meet me at the Roast Beef House on Fifty-second Street on Thursday."

I went to the restaurant for the meeting with Max and Weaver, and I didn't know what was going on. I was looking at the menu, when Weaver said, "Do you want a half hour, an hour, or ninety minutes?"

I thought he was talking about when we were going to order our meal and I said, "A half hour, that's a long time to wait to eat. An hour? Who's going to wait an hour? An hour and a half? That's already crazy when I'm so hungry."

Weaver said, "No. I'm talking about how much air-time you want for the show you and Max are going to do for us."

That's how primitive TV was then, and that's how deals were made. "You want an hour, so OK, I'll give you an hour. You want Friday night at nine? Better, how about Saturday night at eight?"

Max and I had briefly discussed doing the same kind of show he put on at Tamiment, with comedy, songs, and dancing, but when Weaver asked us about how much time we wanted every week on the network, we just didn't know. I looked at Max and I said, "If we're going to go, let's go for broke. Let's take the hour and a half." Max nodded. Neither one of us had any idea of what it entailed. At least *I* didn't. I was on a roll—going nonstop from the Copacabana to the Roxy to *Make Mine Manhattan*—and I honestly was convinced that everything I was going to touch would turn to gold.

It didn't start out that way. First, I nearly was out of the show before it began. It was to be fully sponsored by Admiral, the manufacturer of radio and television sets (automatically giving the series the name "The Admiral Broadway Revue") and it was packaged by Max's agent, William Morris. Wally Jordan of the William Morris office asked me how much I wanted. I said, "A thousand dollars a week." He said, "Out of the question. Nine hundred a week, tops." We argued back and forth and Jordan wouldn't budge. I finally got up and said, "That's it. Thank you. Good-bye." I figured what was the big deal about this television anyway? I could make a thousand a week easy in nightclubs, so if they're trying to chisel me down a lousy hundred dollars, fuck 'em.

When Max heard about this, he nearly hit the ceiling. He went to Jordan and said, "For a hundred dollars a week, you're destroying my production?" Jordan said, "What's the big deal? He's just a comic. We'll go out and hire you another comic." Max said, "Just a *comic*? Don't you realize I've built the whole show around him? No Caesar, no show." Jordan said, "We'll get him the extra hundred."

That's how close it was to my TV career ending stillborn.

So I came back and we started work, with the International Theater, on Columbus Circle, as our studio. In two days, we realized with a thud just what we were up against. How were we going to fill an hour and a half, every week, with fresh material? Nobody had done that before in *any* medium, not even in radio, which still was the big thing.

Fortunately, Max had brought in some very good people who had been with him at Tamiment. There were two very talented writers, Mel Tolkin and Lucille Kallen, who were excellent with sketches. Among the performers were Mary McCarthy and Imogene Coca, a lovely little lady with big brown eyes whom I got to like immediately. I started calling her "Immy," and that's been my name for her ever since.

But what were we going to do? We didn't worry about singing and dancing because Max was a genius at staging production numbers. In between, however, a lot of time had to be filled. We sat around tossing ideas back and forth, and we developed material of what we called the "What if?" category. Someone would say, "What if Christopher Columbus were an usher at the Roxy Theater?" and we'd take it from there, with Columbus navigating people to their seats. Or, "What if Leonardo da Vinci worked as a short-order cook?" and we'd have Leonardo sort of painting sandwiches together like each one was a work of art.

Even so, Max saved us by coming up with two great guest stars for that first show: Gertrude Lawrence and Rex Harrison. We developed a very funny sketch for Harrison and me that became the highlight of the program—and also managed to take up a lot of time. In the first half of the sketch, I was a British clothing salesman waiting on an American customer, played by Harrison. Then we switched roles and Harrison was an American clothing salesman waiting on a British customer, played by me.

This was typical of the crazy ideas that emerged just from Max, Tolkin, Lucille Kallen, and me sitting around a room and tossing notions at each other. It was all verbal, with only Lucille putting anything down on paper. At first, in this particular sketch, we did the orthodox thing and made Harrison the Englishman and me the American. But then I said, "Wouldn't it be funnier and more unexpected if we did it the other way around? I can do a good British accent and Rex's put-on New York accent is hilarious." And that's the way the sketch developed.

I still remember some of the lines:

CAESAR (*as the British clothing salesman*): "You don't *really* want a new suit, sir. The suit you have *on* is gorgeous, stunning. . . . A bowler? No one is wearing bowlers anymore. . . . No, I don't think we have a tie in the store that could suit your exquisite tastes. . . . A collar button? Well, now you have something there, sir. I'll call Kenya. What size collar button do you wear, sir? What color, sir? Might I suggest genuine ivory. Do you want ivory from the tip of the elephant's tusk, or from the base of the tusk. Oh, very good, sir. . . . So veddy sorry, sir. . . . Kenya tells me they're out of collar buttons. But never fear, sir, I'll call Tanganyika and have them shoot an elephant for you.

HARRISON (*as the American clothing salesman*): You say you don't wanna buy a suit today? Now wait a minute, Mac. Here's a deal where you get an extra pair of pants for free, and a tie for free, and a jackknife. And you don't even have to buy a suit to get all that. . . . Just buy the vest. . . . Tell you what I'm gonna do. You buy this beautiful garment, a hunnert percent synthetic pongee, and I'll throw in two tickets to the fights at Madison Square Garden, a box of Havana cigars, and a free week at Olga's Russian Steam Baths. . . . See, what did I tell you? The suit's beautiful. Why am I holding the back of the jacket? We take it in a little, and it fits you perfect.

By our second week on "The Admiral Broadway Revue," we had found our bearings. Basically, it was Max's show. It was the same format he had been using for years at Tamiment and that's what Pat Weaver had bought when he went there to see Max's revues. But we were forced to experiment just to fill the terrible void of those ninety empty minutes we had agreed to occupy every week. Max kept bringing in class acts like Mata and Hari, and Marge and Gower Champion, and I used my old routines, the war-movie number, for example.

Every week, however, we *still* had to come up with new material for the sketches. I began to rely more and more on crazy ideas I got from seeing things on the street and in the subways, and from my relationship with Florence. That's how the "domestic sketches"—the husband and wife conflicts—got started, with me as the husband and Imogene as the wife. Tolkin and Lucille Kallen came in with similar ideas from their own personal experiences. These sketches were just a half-note off, just *slightly* crazy, but close enough to the real thing so that our audiences could recognize facets of their own lives—and laugh about them. In a way, we were making Americans laugh at themselves and their foibles.

It was different. Everything else on television in 1949 was derived from radio and vaudeville. There was the stand-up comedy of Mr. Television, Milton Berle, on "The Texaco Star Theater" with Arnold Stang, Dolores Gray, Bobby Clark, and a lot of old slapstick routines from burlesque. At the other end of the scale, a big hit was "The Aldrich Family," an outgrowth of soft radio situation-comedy.

In that pioneering year, 1949, *we* got to be a big hit, I think, because we were telling outrageous little stories, with plot. Our sketches all had a beginning, a middle, and an end. We weren't just playing for a single punch line. No one

Sid's father, Max, in 1920.

Sid at age two.

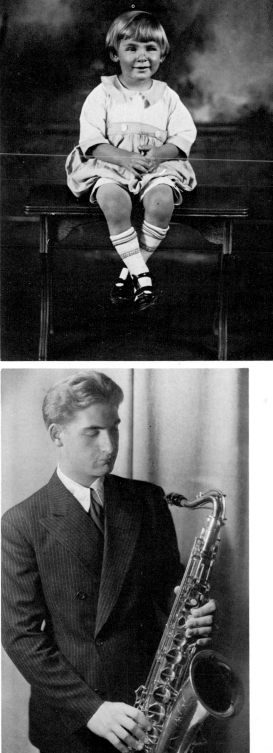

Sid at age five.
Sid at age fifteen, already an accomplished
saxophonist and very serious about music.

Sid *(center)* at the Coast Guard's Brooklyn Barracks, where his show business career really started.

Enter the beauteous Florence, who became Mrs. Caesar in 1943.

Sid flanked by Florence and his mother, Ida.

Another scene from the *Tars and Spars* film.

Sid doing his famous war-movie routine in the
Columbia Pictures movie of *Tars and Spars*, 1946.

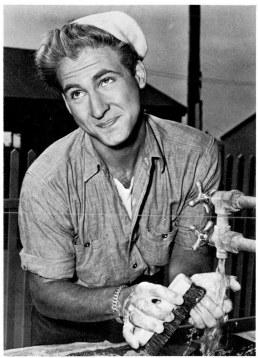

With comedian Julie Oshins
in the huge Broadway hit *Make Mine
Manhattan*, 1948.

Enter producer Max Liebman and "The Admiral Broadway Revue"
on television. This evolved into "Your Show of Shows."

Not impressed is baby Michele (called Shelly) Caesar, with Sid and Florence.

Imogene Coca, a Max Liebman protégée, is an instant perfect match for Sid.

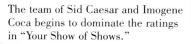

The team of Sid Caesar and Imogene Coca begins to dominate the ratings in "Your Show of Shows."

Along with Carl Reiner...

...and Howard Morris, seen here *(right)* with Carl and Sid, doing one of their most famous routines, The Haircuts, a satire of rock groups.

Sid's funniest character, The Professor, emerges.

Along with the "domestic sketches," The Hickenloopers with Imogene and Sid.

Shelly, Florence, and Sid have now moved to Park Avenue.

Son Rick joins the family.

So the Caesars move to this mansion at King's Point on Long Island.

Living the suburban life, Florence and Sid appear as Cleopatra and Caesar at a local costume ball.

else was doing that—which is why, I believe, we always were at the top or near the top of the ratings. There still were very few television sets in those days and the TV ratings were just an adjunct to the radio ratings. Nevertheless, on a percentage basis, we were doing as well as Jack Benny, Bob Hope and the other big radio stars.

Yet, as successful as we were, suddenly "The Admiral Broadway Revue" was no more. After nineteen weeks, the Admiral Corporation withdrew its sponsorship. And those were the days when, in a carryover from radio network practices, all important television shows had single sponsorship.

Max told me not to worry, and the William Morris Agency booked me into the Empire Room of the Palmer House in Chicago for the summer. Just after I arrived there with Florence (her mother took care of Shelly while we were away), I got a phone call from Ross Siragusa, the president of Admiral, which had its headquarters in Chicago. Siragusa said, "I owe you an explanation, so could you please drop by to see me as soon as you can?" I dropped by to see him the very next afternoon.

The explanation? You won't believe it, but I later checked it out and everything Siragusa told me was true.

Siragusa said: "You're wondering, I'm sure, why we canceled such a popular show. You must understand, Mr. Caesar, that at the time we took on the show, we were selling maybe five hundred to eight hundred television sets a week. After the third week of the show, we had orders for five *thousand* sets a week. It's still going up now. As of today, we have orders for ten thousand sets a week."

Totally baffled, I asked, "So what's so bad?"

Siragusa said, "You've *got* to try to understand, Mr. Caesar. We faced a difficult decision. We have just so much money, and we had to make up our minds whether to put it into capital investment, or to keep putting it into the show. Honestly, we had to put the money into capital investment and retool— just to keep up with the orders."

"What you're telling me," I said, "is that maybe for the first time in history a show is being canceled because it's bringing in too *much* business. We're being dropped because we were too *good*?"

Siragusa broke out into smiles. "I'm so glad you finally *do* understand, Mr. Caesar."

I don't know whether I understood or not, but when I found out that Revlon later had to do the same thing, cutting back its advertising in the exploding new TV medium because it couldn't keep enough of its cosmetics in the stores, I understood.

Anyway, it all became a moot point, because Max Liebman assured me that Admiral or no Admiral, we'd be back on NBC every Saturday night in the fall.

I realized that everything we had done in "The Admiral Broadway Revue" was just prelude, an experimentation period, sort of a warm-up for the main event.

A new era was about to begin.

The Golden Years of "Your Show of Shows."

# 11

# " 'Your Show of Shows' Is Ruining Saturday Night Business on Broadway"

When Florence and I got back to New York at the end of the summer, we met with Max Liebman. Max said to her, "Florence, I want you to know that your husband is going to be a big, big star." Her answer was one of those small, poignant, classic remarks for which she has become famous among our friends. She had finally become worried about my drinking during the last pressure-filled days of "The Admiral Broadway Revue."

Where Have I Been?

My after-work "relaxation" had increased from four or five shots to a full fifth of Scotch before I went home at night. Sensing what lay ahead, she responded to Max's question with, "Couldn't he just be a *little* star?"

As usual, I ignored the implications of what she said and plunged into work on "Your Show of Shows," which was Max's title. Everything seemed the same as "The Admiral Broadway Revue," so we had no idea of the impact we were going to have on American life in the year 1950. We wrote and rehearsed in the same old Nola Studios, across the street from the theater where *Mister Roberts* was playing, and we had only one addition to the cast: talented little second banana Howard Morris, who had worked before with Imogene Coca, and whom Max hired away from the cast of *Gentlemen Prefer Blondes* on Broadway.

Including Max and me, we now had five writers. Number five was Mel Brooks. Actually, he had come with us during the fourth show of "The Admiral Broadway Revue," as the result of a three-year campaign of incredible *chutzpah* and persistence.

Ever since I had worked in the Catskills, I had considered Mel to be sort of a groupie. He was a very poor kid, a Brooklyn neighbor of Don Appel, the man who converted me from a saxophone player to a comedian, and wherever Appel worked in the mountains, you could find little Mel Brooks hanging around. He loved comics and obviously wanted to be one himself. When I opened at the Copacabana, Mel was hanging around. When I opened in *Make Mine Manhattan*, Mel was hanging around. He didn't hang around Milton Berle or Jimmy Durante. He was funny and ingenious and he liked my type of humor, so he hung around me.

When I was in *Make Mine Manhattan*, he came in through

the stage door one night after the show and recognized Max
Liebman. There still was a single spotlight on the stage. Mel
said, "Let me sing a song for you, Max." Without waiting for
an answer, he jumped into the spotlight and sang a lot of
doggerel, ending with "Please love Mel Brooks." Max said
to me, "Who *is* this *meshuggener?*"

When we began "The Admiral Broadway Revue" on television, Mel was still hanging around, but by now, Max was
used to him. While we were preparing the fourth show, we
ran into a crisis just about an hour before air-time. We had
a skit, "The Professor and the Jungle Boy," which definitely
needed something. The Jungle Boy was explaining how he
ordered breakfast back home, and we just couldn't come up
with anything very funny. Finally, we turned to Mel Brooks,
who had been hanging around, hanging around, and we said,
"Do something. Write." Mel came up with a weird sound,
"The Cry of the Crazy Crow," which is what the Jungle Boy
used to order breakfast, and it made the skit hilarious.

So we decided to keep Mel for *shtick* like that, and I asked
him how much money he wanted. He said, "Fifty dollars a
week." I said, "That's unheard of. Let's make it forty." He
said, "No, I need fifty."

I said, "Tell you what I'm gonna do. I'll give you forty-
five, if Max gives you the other five." But Max said no. So
Mel started at forty dollars a week. But after I went downtown
with him and saw where he was living in a cellar on Broome
Street, I relented and raised him to fifty dollars a week.

So Mel was with us when we started the first season of
"Your Show of Shows," but he didn't go on the regular payroll,
or get any credit, for two years.

Mel, by now, has his own version of what happened in
those early years.

## Mel Brooks

*I first met Sid in the Catskills through my friend Don Appel.
Then Don got me a job in another hotel, as a drummer and
the comic, and I kept hearing about Sid, not as a comedian
but as a brilliant tenor saxophonist. I went into the army and
when I came out, I saw the movie* Tars and Spars. *I studied
what Sid did in the picture and I said, "This guy is really
funny,* uniquely *funny."*

*Don Appel took me backstage to see Sid at the Copacabana.
Then, when Sid was playing the Roxy, I went backstage to
see him by myself. I said, "You remember me from Don Appel?"
He said, "Sure, sure." He was stuck in the Roxy for quite some
time because the film was the long-running* Forever Amber,
*and he welcomed company. So I used to go backstage a lot
and I got close to his brothers, Abe and Dave, who usually
were there with him as part of his entourage.*

*I went away in the summer to work in a play called* Separate
Rooms. *I directed it and I starred in it. The play was at the
Mechanic Street Playhouse in Red Bank, New Jersey.*

*When I got back, Sid was in his first rehearsal at the In-
ternational Theater for the soon-to-be-famous "Your Show of
Shows." Sid invited me to come by because he was interested
in my mind and maybe I could help him. I went to the stage
door of the theater. I looked very young, even though I was
out of the army and was twenty-and-a-half years old. I said,
"I'm here to see Sid Caesar. He's a friend of mine and we've
worked together, and he's asked me to come by." His manager,
Leo Pillot, was at the door. Pillot said, "Throw him out." So
these two big ushers picked me up by the scruff of my neck
and the seat of my pants and literally tossed me into the alley.
I said, "You're crazy. You can't do this to Mel Brooks. I'm*

*potentially very important." They were going to call the police,
but Sid heard the scuffle and came down. He said, "He's my
friend. Let him in."*

*Leo just walked away. I think he spotted in me the threat
of a charming, quick-talking guy who could worm his way
into people's affections. He knew I was trouble for him. But I
didn't want to be a personal manager. I just wanted to be a
writer and a comic.*

*So anyway, I went upstairs and we talked for a while, and
Sid told me he was worried about two spots: his monologue,
and a thing called "Airport Interview." In this particular show,
a man in a raincoat was talking to strange people as they got
off airplanes at the airport. I created a character for him right
there, called "Jungle Boy." I told Sid that the interviewer
should ask, "How do you live?" and the Jungle Boy could
illustrate by making this wild sound, pulling a pigeon out of
the air, and eating it. Then I gave him more ideas for "Jungle
Boy" and he offered to pay me fifty dollars a week for ideas.*

*The only animosity I got from the beginning was from Max
Liebman, who saw me as some kind of adventurer and didn't
think I was very talented. I was a street kid and didn't have
any sophistication. Max was a classy guy who wanted to do
a real Broadway revue every week. He wasn't interested in
street humor.*

*It was Sid who recognized that I had a universal concept
of human behavior, but even he couldn't get me on the payroll,
with credit, for a year.*

So much for differences in recollections; but that's what
makes Japanese movies, like *Rashomon*. The important thing
is that Mel Brooks was with us in that first year of "Your
Show of Shows." So was Tony Webster, another fine writer

who had been doing very funny material for the "Bob and Ray" radio show. Except for Max Liebman, who was in his late forties, we were a very young group to shoulder the responsibility of creating what amounted to a full-scale Broadway show every week. I was twenty-seven, just turning twenty-eight, and the others were about my age, apart from Mel Brooks, who was only twenty-one.

Maybe that's why we all were overwhelmed when the show took off like a rocket. Television was spreading through the country very fast that year, and, in a matter of months, we had made an unforeseeable impact on America: we actually changed people's long-standing habits. Instead of the tradition of "going out" on Saturday nights, couples were staying home and watching *us*. NBC got hundreds of thousands of letters from fans, stating just that. The network even had to pacify a delegation of Broadway movie-house owners who went to Pat Weaver and begged him to use his influence to get "Your Show of Shows" switched to the middle of the week, on the grounds that it was ruining their Saturday night business.

The critics were very kind to me personally—even the toughest ones of the day. John Crosby of the *New York Herald Tribune* wrote, "Sid Caesar is one of the wonders of the modern electronic age. He has more funny comedy sequences than he knows what to do with. His routines are even funnier the second time around and he has restored the art of pantomime to the high estate it enjoyed before the talkies and radio." Larry Wolters of the *Chicago Tribune*, who never found much to like in television, wrote, "Sid Caesar doesn't steal jokes; he doesn't borrow ideas or material. A gag is as useless as a fresh situation is to Milton Berle."

I couldn't believe it when I picked up a newspaper one day and read that Alfred Hitchcock was quoted as saying,

"The young Mr. Caesar best approaches the great Chaplin of the early 1920s." That scared me. How could I keep it up? I went to a party once at columnist Leonard Lyons's home, and Margaret Truman, the president's daughter, begged me to do her favorite routine of mine, which was about the thoughts that go through the mind of a six-month-old baby. Later I met General Dwight D. Eisenhower, who was on his way to becoming the *next* president of the United States. He had seen a United Nations sketch in which I had delivered a long speech in my Russian double-talk. The general, who had sat in on many conferences with Soviet officials, asked me where I had learned to speak Russian.

I'm not putting down the performances in "Your Show of Shows"—mine or anyone else's—but the key to our amazing success unquestionably was the writing.

The writing was different by today's standards because what we were doing was live. Modern television people find it difficult to understand what "live" meant, in general. They say, "How long did it take you to do an hour-and-a-half show?"

I say, "An hour and a half."

They say, "No. You don't know what we mean. How long did it take you with the pick-ups, dubbing, fixing the mistakes?"

I say, "There were no pick-ups, dubbing, or fixing mistakes. We just got on the stage and did it."

"But how about titles and things like that?"

"The titles were printed on cards. One camera was focused on the cards, and when we needed a title or a photograph to establish where a skit was taking place, that camera was turned on while the action was continuing onstage."

"But what about costume changes?"

"We did them as best we could, during commercials, and even while something else was going on before the cameras."

"But even so, you really can't mean it when you say it took you exactly an hour and a half to shoot an hour-and-a-half show. What if you ran over and had to cut?"

"Cut what? The air? There was no film, no tape. If, God forbid, we ran over, the network would slice us off in the middle of a sentence and the audience would be watching the next program in the schedule."

"So you really mean you did it in an hour and a half?"

"Yes. An hour and a half. To the second."

There's the same total lack of understanding about what it was like to write for a live variety show in those days. There was no going to the joke books and jotting down gags and sketch-lines in advance. There was no time to think of next week's show, because we were still writing and revising *this* week's show right up until air-time.

We would meet in the writers' room on Monday morning at about ten o'clock, and we hardly ever had a clue as to what we were going to do on the following Saturday night. Someone would begin by saying, "How about a . . . ?" and we'd all start screaming and yelling and discussing it. The place was littered with cigarette butts, partly smoked cigars, and half-empty coffee cups. As each idea was refined, Lucille Kallen made notes. We couldn't use a secretary, who would take down everything, good or bad; a skilled writer like Lucille would record only the acceptable lines we all had hammered out. Mel Brooks and I never did any writing in the accepted sense, with pencil and paper or typewriter. It all came out of our heads and mouths.

By Wednesday night, Lucille's notes finally would be transcribed by a secretary. We had to have *some* sort of script so the director would have an idea of what he was going to have to do. But we never could tell if a routine was going to work until we "put it on its feet." Sometimes, a notion that looked and sounded great on paper was a disaster when it was acted out—first by the writers and then by the actors, in the rehearsal hall—and it had to be discarded. And the material that survived, we kept changing constantly. Even when we got onstage for the actual show, there was improvisation going on. In live television, the improvisation could turn out to be funnier than the original. An interesting example of that was when I was playing an opera singer making himself up in his dressing room. On camera, my brush slipped and I had a black line across my cheek. Without missing a beat, I drew three more lines, in crossed pairs, and I played tic-tac-toe on my face. It got a tremendous laugh.

But to get back to the writing, here's a perfect illustration of how a routine developed, from conception to performance:

I was having a drink in a Greek restaurant one Friday night when I noticed a fly buzzing around the room. The fly settled on a tray of canapes on the table and then zeroed in on a piece of goat's milk cheese. I studied this fly. He kept hopping on that crumb of cheese. I figured he was gloating, "It's mine, all mine," like a guy who gets a brand-new convertible he's wanted for years.

On Monday morning I come into the writers' room and everybody is sitting around looking sick and miserable. Mel Tolkin is staring out the window like he wants to jump out, because Monday is bleeding-to-death day on the show. There's blood all over the floor. So I say, "Fellas, this week I wanna do a fly." They all look nauseated. I say, "Don't throw up because I worked out the psychology of a fly. It could be very funny." I gave them some of my ideas and then I showed them how I could *be* a fly. I started rubbing my wrists, the way a fly keeps washing his claws, or whatever they call his feet. Then I showed them the fly buzzing and whishing through the air. Lucille got interested and came up with something the fly could do. Then Tony Webster chipped in with a fly *shtick*. In another couple of minutes they all agreed it had possibilities and we went to work on it.

By Wednesday, we had a script, which, with a couple of improvisations, is pretty much the way I did the monologue on the air:

*We see him walking, yawning, rubbing himself, cleaning his wings, and murmuring through rounded lips, "Ah, it's morning."*

FLY: Look at the sun coming in through the window. What a house I live in. It's my house. I was so lucky to find this house. Always something to eat. Crumbs on the table, banana peels on the floor, lettuce leaves in the sink. . . . What a nice sloppy house. Well, I'm hungry. I'll see what there is in the sink.

*He folds his insect feet and buzzes to the sink. The sink is empty. Nothing is left on the table. There aren't even any crumbs under the toaster.*

FLY: They cleaned up the house. It's disgusting! They must be expecting guests. . . . Oh, well, why should I aggravate myself? So I'll eat out today. It won't kill me. But I hate restaurants. That greasy food. I can't stand greasy food. I keep slipping off. I can't get a hold on it, and it gets on my wings, makes me sluggish, and I can't fly good.

*On his way to a restaurant, the fly encounters a moth.*


FLY: He's crazy, that guy. Eats wool. Blue serge . . . all that dry stuff. Yugh. And then every night he throws himself against an electric light bulb, knocking his brains out. He's crazy.

*Flying downtown, he is happily humming a song when he suddenly sees a sign that depresses him.*


FLY: Look at that. "Get the new powerful DDT. Kills flies instantly."

*The fly frowns and solemnly remarks: "Oh, my, there's a lot of hatred in the world."*


Expanding within this framework as I went along, this monologue ran for nine minutes when I did it on the air. It worked because houseflies are a fact of everyday life and everyone is familiar with their buzzing and probing. We just took it one ridiculous step further.

"Familiar," "fact of everyday life." Those were the case words for nearly everything we did. We didn't have to rely on the slapstick and pratfalls everyone else was doing in TV comedy. It was a repetition of my going against the trend in the Catskills when I was a teenager.

It's not that difficult to find humor in everyday life—despite what you mostly see *today* on TV. For example, here's our 1950 summary of one of that season's most successful monologues:

Where Have I Been?

Sid is a husband who has just quarreled with his wife and has come to spend the night at a friend's apartment. He enters quietly and then shouts, "*Finished*! Finished, I tell you. *Through*! This is the end!" He agrees with his friend that his wife is a sweet girl, a wonderful girl, considerate and kind, but—he suddenly screws up his face in a mask of uncontrolled rage—"She's *miserable*!" He then proceeds to recount all the indignities his wife has heaped on him. Yet when she phones to apologize at the end of the monologue, he, of course, meekly goes home.

All this time, there is no one on the stage but Sid, but you get the impression of the friend, the friend's wife, the apartment, the telephone, his own wife, his own apartment, everything—just as if they were all there.

In other monologues and solo pantomimes, I was a bashful boy going to his first dance, then the same boy obnoxiously confident at a dance five years later; I was a vain man passing a mirror (I milked that one for five minutes); I was a husband who has had a fight with his wife and suddenly thinks of all the things he should have said in the argument; I was a husband being dragged to a cocktail party he doesn't want to go to; I was an expectant father getting incensed about what a brat and monster his yet-to-be-born child was going to be (a satire on the Soliloquy in *Carousel*); I was a bridegroom walking down the aisle thinking gloomily about his future as a married man.

In one very funny solo skit, I was a man getting his boss hopelessly lost trying to direct him to his house by telephone. Finally I say, "Where are you *now*? . . . Well, you're an American citizen. They've *got* to let you back into the country."

Just that little one-step crossover from the everyday to the ridiculous.

It was the same with the skits I did with Imogene. Some of the best of those were what we simply called "Clichés." The idea for this category came from Imogene herself. She had a habit of talking in clichés in real life, and one day when we were kidding her about them, she said, "I admit I shouldn't do it, but a lot of people do, so why not a series of skits about a couple of people who speak in platitudes all the time?"

And so we had a father and mother taking their children to school for the first time and mouthing all the clichés that parents will at such a time. We did the clichés of two superstitious people pretending not to be superstitious; also those of a pair of strangers who meet while waiting in line outside a movie theater. One of the funniest lines we ever did in a cliché skit was when Imogene and I were discussing the use of psychology in bringing up children today. Lucille Kallen came up with the following gem:

IMOGENE: I think the old method of spanking a child is passé.
SID: I say don't just spank a child. Talk to the child, reason with him, find out what's on his mind. And when you find out the reason, the real cause—*then* belt him.

Again, humor springing from real, everyday events. We didn't have to knock down a fire hydrant with a car and cause a geyser of water, which seems to be the standard type of laugh-getter in so many so-called comedy movies of today.

A lot of our humor was a mixture of the sad and the funny. Charlie Chaplin knew that in 1910 and we knew it in 1950. A guy who's in trouble is a very funny guy. A man who's got enough money to pay the rent, there's nothing funny about

103

him. You've got to be involved with and worried about the person you're going to laugh at, or cry at.

In so many of my routines, I played the goat—a seemingly cocky, self-assured guy who really is very insecure and keeps screwing up. I didn't mind being the slob in any skit that we wrote for a guest star. When I was the downtrodden fellow, even the loser in all his fights with his wife, any turnaround, any small triumph by my character, got big laughs from the audience—which sympathized with me. Playing a downtrodden fellow was not easy for me. It called on all my acting skills because I'm so big and strong-looking. Nearly all the other comedians who have used this technique of extracting humor out of being a little guy failing and succeeding have been little guys themselves, physically that is.

I used to love to do sad little guys, *schleppers*, in monologues about inanimate objects. Remember my number in the Coast Guard, in which I played a battered penny gumball machine who finally, through dishonesty, was promoted to be a twenty-five-cent slot machine? I did a lot more like that on "Your Show of Shows." One that is remembered by a lot of people was "The Whitewall Tire." I played this tire, who started life very proudly on a wheel of a Rolls-Royce. But then he gets thrown out when his usefulness is over and he goes through all kinds of terrible experiences before he finally ends up in a dump, with only his memories of the good old days. The audience actually laughs and cheers when he's picked up by a kid and regains his dignity as a backyard swing.

A human being playing the part of a tire? It sounds ridiculous that audiences could believe me. But they did. That's because even the inanimate-object sketches came out of reality. Haven't *you* ever wondered sadly about the fate of a favorite old car you had to trade in?

Realism. The facts of everyday life. That was the key to the most bizarre of our characters: The Professor, with his squashed-in top hat, disreputable looking tailcoat, and tie askew. He may *look* bizarre, but who can't identify someone just like him in real life—a man who pretends to know everything but knows nothing.

The Professor was a long time developing. We started out with what we called "Nonentities in the News." This was the reporter in a trenchcoat, interviewing a strange character deplaning at the airport. The reporter originally was someone from the cast, usually Tom Avera. The Deplaning Strange Character always was Sid Caesar. I was Jungle Boy, I was self-proclaimed experts from Russia and France, I was Dr. Spaghetti, telling how to cook and eat various kinds of pasta. Some of these characters remained because, in order to spare ourselves, we were desperately trying to come up with regular spots we could do every week.

Out of all these Deplaners emerged the most interesting and long-lasting character of all—the preposterous Professor, expert in *all* subjects, the fraudulent know-it-all with a German accent.

Everyone I know has a favorite Professor routine.

Here's the script of one that's typical of what I did with him in the early days:

INTERVIEWER: Doctor, would you explain to the audience in simple language the basis for your theory of sleep?

PROFESSOR VON SEDATIVE: Yah. Schleep is vunderbar. Schleep is beautiful. But schleep is no good to you if you is vide avake. . . . I haff a friend vunce, he could schleep anyveres. In der boiler factory, in der foundry, in a shtockyard. He could go on a train and right avay he fall aschleep. Pass all the stations.

Where Have I Been?

> INTERVIEWER: That's wonderful.
> PROFESSOR VON SEDATIVE: It was lousy. He was the engineer. He wrecked more trains, dot friend of mine.

But The Professor—and many other things—began to flower on "Your Show of Shows" with the addition of Carl Reiner in that first season.

# 12

## "Sidney, You Need a Psychiatrist"

We had needed a straight man ever since we began with "The Admiral Broadway Revue," but Max Liebman was dedicated to some very fixed ideas, one of which was that a straight man always has to be taller than the comic. *Why* the straight man always has to be taller than the comic, I'll never know. Maybe the concept goes all the way back to Rosencrantz and Guildenstern in Shakespeare's times, maybe it just goes back to burlesque; maybe Max was starting his own handbook on what makes successful comedy. Anyway, with him, it was an immutable law that the straight man has to be taller than the comic.

This made it difficult for us, since I am six feet one. God forbid, a fine actor would show up and he was only five feet eleven. Max would just tell him how good he was and express regrets that he couldn't be stretched on the rack for maybe three inches.

Then, fortunately, Carl Reiner came along. He is six two.

I think it would be better to let Carl explain in his own words just how he came to join us.

## Carl Reiner

*I came from another world. I had been in the army, doing shows overseas, and only when I got back after the war did I see the movie version of* Tars and Spars. *I watched Sid in the film and I said, "Wow, this is it." But our paths never crossed. I was the Top Banana in* Call Me Mister *on Broadway, and then, while Sid was doing "The Admiral Broadway Revue" on NBC, I starred in the competing CBS show, "54th Street Revue." I used to watch the Admiral show and say to myself, "I belong with that group." I didn't know it then, but Sid also was watching me in the CBS show and remembered me.*

*I left "54th Street Revue," saying, "Let me out of this television shit," when I was offered a part in a stage production,* Pretty Penny, *directed by George S. Kaufman, with sketches by Jerome Chodorov and dances by Michael Kidd. I then went into another stage revue,* Alive and Kicking, *which began to develop problems. Who should be called in as a play doctor but Max Liebman.*

*The first thing he asked me was how tall I was. Then he had me meet with him and Sid. Sid told me how much he*

108

*had liked my work in "54th Street Revue" and asked if I would mind coming on "Your Shows of Shows" to be a foil for him. He was very nice about it. He knew I had credentials as a Top Banana. I said, "I'd love it. I belong there. With you, I'd be very happy to be a Second Banana."*

*I really meant it. I had such great respect for his talent that I felt there's nothing he does that I do, that he can't do better. For example, I used foreign-language double-talk in my night-club act. No match for Sid's. But I decided to turn that to my advantage soon after I joined the show. I was miserable at first. The writers all were crammed into Max's office, some of them overflowing into the toilet, and the actors all had to wait out in the hall. We were only called in when there was something to rehearse. I decided I had to get out of the hall and into the inner office. So I began to suggest things.*

*The first thing I suggested was that since I could do French double-talk—though not as well as Sid—maybe we could do a spoof of a French movie with a cast (until then, Sid had been doing foreign films alone, as monologues, playing all the parts himself). I demonstrated by doing the ritual of a Frenchman lighting a cigarette. Sid laughed and joined in, and we went back and forth, and the writers joined in, and soon they had come up with a very funny routine, which was used in that week's show.*

*I had worked myself into the inner room.*

With the addition of Carl, our ensemble was complete. There were four of us who blended beautifully—Imogene, Carl, Howard Morris, and me—and we could greatly extend the range of our skits with a lot of people. For example, we could bring in wives for Carl and Howard, if need be, in our so-called "domestic sketches" about the funny interactions of married couples. Imogene, of course, always was *my* wife.

The show became more diverse—and better. Max began to add classical artists to his musical numbers. He brought in another topflight writer, Joe Stein, who later became famous for his *Fiddler on the Roof*.

We really were in high gear now.

Here, for example, is an instance of how neatly Carl fitted into the Charlie and Doris Hickenlooper "domestic sketches" that Imogene and I did together.

*Doris, in her never-ending quest to make Charlie appreciate "the finer things," is steering him into an exotic East Indian restaurant. The maître d' is Carl.*

REINER (*bowing*): The ancient house of the Golden Lamb is your servant, O honored guests. May the grass grow tall for the goats of your father's father, and your children drink the wine of abundance that grows as the grapes on the vine of your mother's mother. . . .

CAESAR (*rising with clenched fist*): I ought to belt you.

*Caesar and Coca struggle with the offerings on the menu.*

CAESAR: What have you got to eat?

REINER: Klochmoloppi. We also have lich lop, slop lom, shtocklock, rishkosh, and flocklish.

CAESAR: Yuch!

REINER: We have yuch, too. Boiled or broiled?

Imogene and I, of course, went on to have a terrible fight over the exotic food, with Carl standing smugly and taciturnly by.

110

In the other sketches, the onscreen team meshed beautifully with the off-screen team, as in a hospital drama we did called "Emergency." Carl was the tough, do-it-by-the-book chief medical officer, I was the idealistic young surgeon, and Howard Morris was my adoring physician-sidekick.

> REINER (*sternly*): Dr. Hamilton, I must make it clear to you that we will countenance no experimental medicine around here while I am in charge of this hospital.
>
> CAESAR (*with stirring music behind him*): When I took that Hippocritical Oath, I didn't take it as a hypocrite— others may be hypocrites about the Hippocritical Oath, but if hypocrites meant that hypocritically speaking, sir, I'm hip and no hypocrite is going to tell me—and I'm also hip to a lot of things that go on around here.

*A mysterious new patient is brought in: Imogene. She is suffering from amnesia.*

> MORRIS: Please try as hard as you can to remember something from your personal life. All you seem to have on your mind is dog-food commercials.
>
> IMOGENE: Nippy dog food tastes so great/ Makes your puppy glad he ate/ Full of precious vitamins/ Look for Nippy in the big red tins/ I like Nippy, woof, woof, woof.
>
> MORRIS (*to Caesar*): Looks hopeless, Dr. Hamilton. Why don't you try a word association test with her?
>
> CAESAR: Bread.
>
> COCA: Butter.
>
> CAESAR: Hickory.
>
> COCA: Dickory.
>
> CAESAR: Dock.
>
> COCA: The mouse.

CAESAR: Ran up.

COCA: The clock.

CAESAR: The clock, the clock . . .

COCA: The clock.

CAESAR (*intensely, onto a lead*): What *about* the clock?

COCA (*very pleased with herself*): The clock struck one, and down he run. Hickory dickory dock! Hurray!

Howard and I decide to try an experimental drug on Imogene, and Carl strips me of my medical rank, like a military officer who has been court-martialed. He takes away my stethoscope and prescription pad. He breaks my tongue-depressor in two.

CARL: You've depressed your last tongue.

Nevertheless, I persist, without authorization. Howard helps me. I explain the procedure to him.

CAESAR: The first phase is to inject the patient with twenty cc's of silio helium. And ninety-eight cc's of mindo-mycin. . . . And then we apply my memory pusher to the arm of the patient and exert pressure of tremendous force so that the mind is pushed from the subconscious into the conscious. But we have to be careful. . . . If we apply too much pressure, she might blow her top. . . . Then we lower the patient into a tank of water, because when a person is drowning, her whole life flashes before her eyes.

We lower Imogene into the tank of water. The first time, she comes up spluttering.

CAESAR: OK, now, who are you?
COCA: Esther Williams.

The next time she comes up for air, she thinks she's Johnny Weissmuller. The third time, it works:

COCA: I'm Hilda Frankenheimer, and I live at 226 Canal Street, and I'm employed at the Chi Chi Hat Company in Paterson, New Jersey.

I thank her for having faith in my experimental medicine, and she thanks me for saving her life, spritzing water all over me as we embrace at the end of the skit.

With Carl as the interviewer, the Professor skits got progressively better, too. In one of our more highly acclaimed ones, the all-knowing Professor is a mountain-climbing expert:

CARL: In your book on mountain climbing, I was most interested in your chapter on falling.
CAESAR: Absolutely. If you want to be a mountain climber, the first thing you gotta know is how to fall. Just like you want to be a swimmer, the first thing you gotta know is how to get wet. The same thing applies. You climb mountains, you're not always gonna be up there.
CARL: Professor, supposing you're twenty-five thousand feet up on the sheer side of a mountain, and your safety belt snaps. Is there anything you can do?
CAESAR: Well, you got two seconds. And I mean, that's it. Don't hang around. Immediately you see the rope snap, and I mean immediately, you right away fill your lungs

with air . . . and you start to scream. And you keep
screaming all the vay down.

CARL: But why do you keep screaming?

CAESAR: Dummkopf! So they know where to find you.

CARL: Is that the only thing you can do, Professor? Is there
any other alternative?

CAESAR: Yes. Again, you got two seconds. Immediately
you see that rope snap, immediately you spread your
arms . . . and you start to fly as far as you can.

CARL: But Professor, man can't fly.

CAESAR: How do you know? You may be the first one, boy.
You got nothin' to lose. You could always go back to
screaming.

CARL: Which method do you use, Professor?

CAESAR: Me, I'm a flying screamer. I fly, I scream, I fly,
I scream. . . . Why? Because I hate to fly.

Also, with Carl, we had a far greater range with what we
could do in our satires of movies. Every new film that came
along was fair game for us. We did spoofs of *High Noon*, *A
Streetcar Named Desire*, *On the Waterfront*, and a dozen others.
One of my favorites was our version of *Shane*, which we called
"Strange."

As in the original, a mysterious stranger shows up at a
remote farm in the Old West. The farmer is Howard Morris;
his young son is Imogene Coca. I am the stranger. I ask for
a drink of water and swallow one gallon after another from
the well.

MORRIS: You seem mighty thirsty, stranger. Have a long
dry ride?

CAESAR: No. Had a herring for breakfast.

MORRIS: What's your name?

CAESAR: Folks call me . . . Strange.

MORRIS: "Strange"? What's your first name?

CAESAR: Very. But you can call me Strange.

COCA (*who has been admiring him*): Gee, that's a nice gun, Strange. That's a nice holster, Strange. Nice gun-belt, Strange. I like you, Strange. You got nice boots, Strange. You're nice, Strange.

CAESAR: Get away, kid, or I'll blast you.

I move in with the family when I learn that they're being persecuted by Barton, a gunslinger dressed all in black and played by Carl Reiner.

MORRIS: Why are you staying here? You hardly know us. Why are you risking your life for us?

CAESAR: Cuz they're the bad guys and I'm the good guys, that's why.

The kid (Coca) continues to idol-worship me, and I have the inevitable showdown with the villain (Reiner).

REINER: You know what you are? You're a lily-livered, lemon-and-lime lollipop lickin' sodbuster.

CAESAR: Did you call me a lily-livered, lemon-and-lime lollipop lickin' sodbuster?

REINER: You're a low-down, lip-eared, lily-livered lemon-and-lime lollipop lickin' sodbuster.

There are more confrontations, leading up to the big gunfight. Only I forget to bring my gun to the gunfight. The kid throws me my gun. I shoot all six of Barton's henchmen.

REINER (*triumphant*): Six shots. Six bullets. You're empty.

I shoot again and Barton falls. Carl has an unbelieving look on his face.

CAESAR: The only seven-shooter in the West. Made it myself.

My mission accomplished, I ride off into the sunset, as mysteriously as I have arrived.

COCA: Come back, Strange. Strange, come back. Strange
   (*echo*) . . . Strange (*echo*) . . . Strange (*echo*) . . .
CAESAR (*from a distance*): Shut up, you rotten kid (*echo*) . . .
   rotten kid (*echo*) . . . rotten kid (*echo*). . . .

Some critics wrote that they liked our spoof better than the original *Shane* with Alan Ladd.

I should have been a very happy man. I was making four thousand dollars a week, thirty-nine weeks a year; I was able to move my family to Forest Hills and then to Park Avenue; I was receiving all sorts of honors, inside the industry and out. Why, then, was I continuing my increasingly heavy boozing?

The easy excuse, as before, was the unrelenting pressure of the work I was doing, week after week. I had no conception of the forces that were pulling me apart inside. Externally, I was trying to copy all the trappings of success that were important to my father. A successful man smoked foot-long cigars, went to the steam baths, drove the biggest possible car, wore hand-tailored suits, ordered double steaks in restaurants, and drank the most expensive top-brand-name Scotch whisky. I was still bound by the old immigrant ethic of the 1920s.

I prided myself on never being drunk at work. The booze came after we were finished for the day. It got so that I was afraid to drive myself home, so I acquired a huge limousine and a chauffeur named Tony. Tony would drive me the few blocks from our apartment at Eighty-first Street and Park Avenue to the show's new headquarters at the City Center Theater on West Fifty-fifth Street—and then back home again at night. After a while, he'd even drive me one block when I had to go to my doctor. Florence kept sending me to the doctor. She didn't know what to do. Neither did the doctor.

The doctor seemed mostly worried about my weight. I had ballooned up to 240 pounds. Diets the doctor understood; alcoholism wasn't even considered a disease in those days. So he put me on diets and I ignored them. My gluttony was typical of all my excesses at that stage of my life. Every Saturday night, when the show went off the air, my brothers Abe and Dave would have a huge triple-decker corned beef-pastrami-chopped liver sandwich waiting for me in my dressing room. (Both Abe and Dave worked for me; it was another subconscious emulation of my father, for whom they had previously worked.) I'd wolf down the sandwich, followed by a couple of tumblers of Scotch, after which I'd usually throw up.

Then I'd be ready for the postshow cast party at Danny's Hideaway. Tony would drive me over there and I'd have a couple of snorts in the limousine. At the restaurant, I'd always order not one but two steaks, with baked potatoes and all the side dishes. I'd drink myself to near unconsciousness, throw up again, and then Tony would take me home.

I threw up a lot in those days. It probably saved my life.

At least it kept a lot of the alcohol from reaching my liver and pancreas. The vomiting also caused me a lot of embarrassment. Carl Reiner tells how one night in Lindy's restaurant, I rushed from our table to the men's room to throw up. I didn't make it. Instead, I splattered all over little Leo Lindy, who was recovering from an illness and hobbling about with a cane. As Carl tells it, poor Leo looked up at him and said plaintively, "And I thought Sid liked me."

The whiskey also caused the underlying anger and violence in me to emerge. That was the case in the situation where I nearly killed Mel Brooks. I was in Chicago on hiatus, doing a stage show at the Chicago Theater on State Street. Mel and my brother Dave were with me. The city was filled with Shriners having their convention. They made up most of the audience while I was working at the theater one night. They were fooling around and making noise and no one could hear me. I got enraged, and when I walked off the stage, I immediately hit the bottle.

We went back to our hotel, the Palmer House. I was still furious and I continued drinking. Mel and Dave watched television for a while. Then Mel said, "I don't want to sit around all night looking at you drinking Scotch. Let's go out."

Without realizing what I was doing, I got to my feet and walked over to the window. I opened it and looked down at the traffic, eighteen floors below. Then I walked over and grabbed Mel. I said, "You want out? I'll *show* you out." I lifted him off his feet and rushed him to the window, dangling him so that he was half in and half out.

Just then, Dave grabbed both me *and* Mel with his huge arms. Dave weighed 300 pounds, so he was able to handle the two of us. He pulled us back in the room. He said to me,

"Do you realize what you nearly just did, you crazy son-of-a-bitch?"

I was so out of it, I didn't have the vaguest idea.

Another time in Chicago, Florence and I were in a tiny elevator at a nightclub called the Chez Paree. There was a man in the elevator who said to Florence, "When you look at me, sweetheart, smile." It didn't occur to me that some rough customers hung out at the Chez Paree. I sank my fist into the man's stomach, nearly feeling his spine at the far side, and held him up until we reached the ground floor. I let him drop and gave five dollars to the frightened little elevator operator, saying, "I think this gentleman has had too much to drink." In a similar elevator incident, I pinched a man's collarbone so hard that blood ran out onto his shirt. I told his companions, "Your friend has been drinking too much cranberry juice. It's leaking."

There were several incidents when New York taxi drivers made rude remarks and I separated them from their cabs. One such scene took place outside Cafe Society in Greenwich Village, where I had gone to see Zero Mostel perform. I grabbed the man by his lapels and pulled him through his side window before, once again, Dave stopped me. A second time, in front of the Roxy Theater, a taxi driver came out of the door of his cab. Only the door was not open. It *became* open.

I was a bad drunk. I was very aggressive at parties. I had a big mouth. People put up with it because of who I was. I still don't know why Florence did. Frequently I'd take my anger out on her and abuse her verbally, not physically. Everything was her fault. I guess she figured that I was in a passing phase and would change. And I *did* change, but only because I had sense enough to realize when I had gone too far. Then I'd be apologetic and contrite for a few days, and try to make her know how much I needed her. And she would forgive me.

During hiatus in 1951, we decided to spend the summer on a nine-week tour of Europe. I'd relax, see the sights, have a few laughs—and get back to my old self. We paid for the entire trip in advance, several thousand dollars.

We were to leave on the beautiful French ocean liner, the *Liberté,* but at the last minute, there was a big argument between my lawyers and NBC about my contract with the network for the following season. The deal finally was settled in the bathroom of our stateroom just before the ship was to sail. It wasn't a very good start for a relaxing vacation.

Florence and I got to Southampton and took the boat train directly to Paris. I managed not to drink too much all this time, to be sure to make it pleasant for her.

In Paris, we checked into the Hotel George V. We had a beautiful suite, but I felt terribly uncomfortable. After all the recognition back home, here nobody knew me. Also, I felt lost not being able to speak the language. Maybe I thought I'd be able to get by with my double-talk French. With the concierge and the waiters at the George V, it didn't work. All I heard from *them* was real English, in snotty tones, and even double-talk English, in snotty tones.

On the third day of our nine-week European tour, we decided to go to the Grand Prix at Longchamp outside Paris. We had trouble finding our way there, and even though everything had been set up for us in advance, no one at the racetrack knew who I was. Unable to speak French, we couldn't even find our seats.

The anger surged up in me and I said to Florence, "We're going home."

She said, "To the hotel?"

I said, "No. To New York."

We flew back, having blown all the prepaid money we had laid out for the trip.

Not long after that, Florence said, "Sidney, you need a psychiatrist."

Not yet. Later.

Instead, I went to my internist, who gave me a drug to wean me off the booze. It was chloral hydrate. Naturally, I took it *with* the booze.

That's the combination that killed Marilyn Monroe.

# 13
## It Was Like *Stella Dallas*

The sedative-alcohol duo did not seem to affect me—at first. I continued to take neither during the day, when I had to call on all my creative and performing powers. At night, I needed desperately to sleep, in order to unwind from the pressures of doing the show and to forget all my many fears of failing. What I really wanted was oblivion. The drug, plus the booze, certainly provided that. Florence and I both were misguided. As indomitable and supportive as Florence was, she actually welcomed the fact that I would come home and almost immediately fall asleep—sometimes at the dinner table. "It was better," she says, "than having to put up with your belligerence and nastiness." Little did she know.

Our baby, Shelly, knew nothing, of course—except that I

wasn't around very much. One day, I happened to be home when she got back from nursery school. She said, "Daddy, what is your name?"

I said, "Sweetheart, what does Mommy call me?"

She said, "Sid or Sidney."

I said, "Does that answer your question, darling?"

She said, "No. What is your *last* name?"

I said, "My last name is the same as your last name. What do they call you at school?"

She said, "Michele Caesar."

Realization dawned on her pretty little face.

"Oh," she said, "then you're the Sid Caesar who everybody watches on television."

Our second child, Rick, was born in 1952. Today, he is six feet eleven and a doctor, practicing emergency room medicine at the University of Oregon Medical Center in Portland. Though he was an infant when I began my drug-alcohol addiction, he became aware of my problem earlier than Shelly did. As my only son, he also became the victim of my frustrations when he deviated even slightly from what I expected of him. As an adult, and as a physician, he still marvels at the fact that I survived what he usually sees as death-on-arrival cases, DOA's, in his hospital emergency room.

When Rick was born, we hired a baby-nurse to take care of him. She was a lovely older Jamaican lady named Maranee Harvey, who had been a schoolteacher in her native country. Maranee stayed on with us and has been our loyal and devoted housekeeper for thirty years. She became a second mother to me, and alone or with Florence, was responsible for keeping me alive in the dark days.

Once, for example, I came home from work when Florence was visiting friends and Maranee was alone in the house. She

123

Where Have I Been?

is a little woman, only five feet tall, but she stood up to me and really chewed me out for obviously being smashed. I was reeking with vomit and she made me go into the bathroom to take off my clothes and clean myself up.

But let Maranee tell the rest of the story.


## Maranee Harvey

*Mr. Caesar went into the bathroom, like I told him, and I heard the water running. While I was trying to get Mrs. Caesar on the phone, I heard a fearful crash. I ran to the bathroom and knocked. Mr. Caesar didn't answer.*

*The door wasn't locked, and something made me open it. There was Mr. Caesar, lying on the floor unconscious. He had passed out. He was stark naked and I am a very Christian woman, but I didn't like the way his head was pushed forward onto his chest. His breathing was very loud, leaving me frightened that if I left him that way, he might choke to death.*

*So even though he didn't have a stitch of clothes on, I overcame my religious scruples and dragged him out of the bathroom by his feet. He was very heavy then, weighing well over 200 pounds, and it was not an easy task for me.*

*When I finally was able to pull him onto a carpeted portion of his dressing room, I rearranged his head so there was no more danger of his strangling. Then covered him with blankets. Fortunately Mrs. Caesar soon came home. Between the two of us, we managed to lift him up onto his bed.*

Incredible as it seems, such occurrences did not hurt my performance on "Your Show of Shows." I must have had the constitution of an ox. I'd just sleep off every incident and be ready for work the next day.

The show kept getting better and better. With the addition of Carl Reiner to the cast, we had a full-fledged repertory company, but the repertory material still kept coming out of the heads of me and the writers. We all were upwardly-mobile young people, typical of a lot of the post-World War II population, so we were able to spot satire-worthy situations all around us. One of the writers would come in on Monday morning and say, "Boy, did I have an experience at a party last night. A guy and his wife started fighting because she had smashed their car into a funeral home, and he just found out she also forgot to pay the auto insurance premium." By the end of the day, we had hammered out a skit for me and Imogene, based on that situation.

A lot of *my* ideas came from foreign movies and silent movies, which Florence first had introduced me to. Every Friday afternoon at four o'clock, I'd still take time off from preparing the show and go to see films with her at The Museum of Modern Art. That's how I got the notion for a routine that many people still remember. I saw the old German silent movie *The Last Laugh* with Emil Jannings, in which he played an army general who ended his days working as a doorman. So we developed a skit in which I am a German general being dressed by my orderly, Howard Morris—with boots, tunic, epaulettes, medals, the whole shot. The audience thinks I'm going to a cabinet meeting, at the very least, but only in the last scene does it become apparent I'm just going out to whistle up cabs and open car doors.

Anything that moved became a target for me to do. In one old film, I saw a Bavarian belfry clock with human-sized doll figures coming out to strike the hour, using sledgehammers and anvils and God knows what else. Then I saw a similar belfry in a film about the Piazzo San Marco in Venice. I began to sense the humorous possibilities in what might happen if the medieval mechanism got screwed up and the figures began hitting each other, instead of the anvils. I suggested the idea at the writers' meeting one day, and one of our most famous routines resulted, with Imogene, Howard, Carl, and me miming the figures in the belfry.

Those writers' meetings were wild affairs. Everybody came in looking very scruffy. On the other hand, I always wore a suit with a tie and even a vest. I thought such an outfit made me the authority figure, which I was anyway since mine was the last word in any argument about the script. Only Max Liebman now had a veto over my decisions, but he rarely was in writers' conferences with us and rarely exercised his veto—except possibly to cut time from our sketches to extend his musical numbers.

The writers battled and screamed over nearly every sentence that went into every script. On occasion, they even threw punches. Mel Brooks exasperated them all because he would sit around, coolly reading the *Wall Street Journal*, and then come in with the one punch line we all were searching for. Mel's childhood nickname was Mibbie, so we had a Mibbie doll, with which Mel could be hanged in effigy when he exasperated the others.

Most of the exasperation came from Mel's habit of always being late. He also had an annoying fixed routine, *after* he came in late. He could not begin work, he said, until he had had his buttered bagel, which was sent in by a nearby delicatessen every morning.

One day the bagel arrived before Mel did and I paid for it. When Mel finally showed up, I told him he owed me twenty dollars. He screamed, "For *what?*"

I said, "For your bagel."

He said, "But a bagel is only twenty-five cents."

I said, "That's right. I gave the delivery boy twenty-five cents for the bagel and a nineteen-dollar-and-seventy-five-cent tip."

The ploy did not work. Mel *still* kept coming in late.

But he also was indefatigable in trying to sell his ideas to me. He once got so excited about one of his skits that he followed me down the street trying to convince me to use it. When I continued to resist, he actually threw a punch at me, poking me in the chest. I looked at this little guy, whom I could have squashed, and I said, "Mel, I will let you live." Then I added, "If you feel *that* strongly about your idea, I'll use it."

Mel had another ingenious technique. Every Saturday, just before air-time for the show, I'd always take a one-hour nap in my dressing room with the door closed. No one was supposed to disturb me. But Mel would come by, open the door a crack, and whisper some of his favorite lines, which we had discarded in the writers' meeting. He was hoping to get through to my mind subliminally—and once or twice he succeeded.

Nearly all the crazy things that happened involved Mel Brooks. Just before Christmas, he and Howard Morris were leaving our rehearsal quarters in City Center. As they got to the bottom of the stairs, Mel said to Howard, "Stick 'em up." Howard thought Mel had gone insane, but then Mel said ominously, "Give me your wallet, or I'll beat the shit out of you." Howard turned over his wallet. Mel gave it back to him the next day, as his Christmas present.

The same thing happened, in a different form, the following year. Mel and Howard were rowing on the lake in Central Park, when Mel said, "Give me your wallet, or I'll throw you in the water and drown you." Once again, Howard turned over his wallet to Mel, who once again gave it back to him as his Christmas present.

The show was a continuing success. I was awarded my first Emmy on February 18, 1952—the day my son, Rick, was born—and the awards came in clusters after that, not only for me but for the others and for the production itself. Since Max Liebman and I believed that writing was the key to everything else, our writers got the highest pay in the industry. Max added Neil Simon (we all called him "Doc") and his talented brother, Danny Simon.

My attorney, Milton Mound, kept negotiating salary increases for me. I ended up earning twenty-five thousand dollars a show, thirty-nine shows a year—which amounted to just less than a million dollars annually. Those figures were unheard of in show business in those days. I don't think that even Clark Gable made that much. Was I worth it? I kept asking myself that disturbing question over and over again. Out of guilt, I guess, I spread my money around obsessively. In the era of the two-dollar tip, I never gave less than twenty dollars. My brother Abe was on the payroll, getting a handsome salary for taking care of my fan mail. My brother Dave was on the payroll, getting a handsome salary for doing bit parts in the show and acting as our voice-of-the-people consultant in our writers' meetings (if Dave nodded when we talked out a skit, the voice of the people had spoken in favor of it; if Dave shook his head, it was thumbs down). Dave also maintained a table of candy and other snacks for the writers.

I added to our household staff at home; I made a lot of tailors wealthy by constantly ordering handmade suits with the broadest-possible padded shoulders; I was the joy of the tobacconists who imported my cigars from Cuba. Florence had sense enough to try to slow down my spending, but she couldn't. Her early Socialist leanings made her resent the fact that I put a limousine and a chauffeur at her disposal to help her do her shopping. She used to try to duck the chauffeur so she could rummage happily through the bargain tables at working-people's stores like Ohrbach's—the way she once did with her mother.

The money I was making at the age of thirty-two was ridiculous, and even disturbing to me. There was the old gnawing fear that all this had come too fast and too easily. There was something wrong with the equation. Yet, I was defensive about it.

One day, for example, I was called in to have dinner with General David Sarnoff, chairman of the board of RCA, which is NBC's parent company. I went to his office and we had a wonderful meal, at the end of which he said, kind of puzzled, "Do you know that you make ten times more than my top scientist down at our research laboratories in Camden, New Jersey?"

I said, "Well, General, you have a great tank, the fastest, best-armored, with the most accurate gun, but if you don't have a driver, the tank doesn't go anywhere."

The General said, "A driver I can always get."

I said, "Ah, but can he shoot, too?"

The General looked thoughtful, nodded, and changed the subject.

I must have seemed real cocky then, but I wasn't. I never knew when I would look up and suddenly there would be no hands on the carriage. In my ignorance, I never related my drinking and pill-taking to my insecurities. I was a drinker, I thought, but not an alcoholic. I took pills, but how could

I be an addict? After all, I could get up in the morning and be totally productive. The curse of my booze excesses in those days was that I never had a hangover. If I had, at least I would have felt I was being punished for doing something wrong.

Instead, I found other ways of punishing myself. The guilts from the past, for example. Some of them were not my fault. One of the most devastating experiences of my life came one night when I was doing a benefit at the Waldorf-Astoria. When it was over, I came out of the hotel and started to get into one of the fourteen limousines lined up for my entourage. It was snowing. I looked across Park Avenue, and through the snowflakes, I could make out the figure of a woman, leaning against a lamppost. I looked closer and said to Dave, "My God, that's Ma." I couldn't believe it. It was like a surreal silent movie. It was like *Stella Dallas*.

I walked across the street. I said, "Ma, you're standing in the snow under a lamppost, looking across the street at your son coming out of the Waldorf-Astoria, with a tuxedo and a limousine? Why didn't you just come with Dave?"

She said, "No, I didn't want to bother you."

I said, "Ma, so you're here, but at least come across the street and I'll send you home in one of the limousines."

She said, "No, it's all right. I'll take the subway home to Yonkers." And she walked away into the night. I yelled for Dave and we tried to find her, but we couldn't. I didn't blame her. She didn't know what she was doing. By her standards, she thought she was doing right. But she succeeded in laying a guilt-trip on me that I didn't get over for years. Especially when she died not long after that.

The guilts I couldn't handle, but at least I made some attempt to control my unreasonable rages. And like my previous episodes of violence, they *were* unreasonable—as I now well know. A scene designer on the show would come in with something I didn't like and I'd tear it up with my bare hands. A horse once threw Florence while we were out riding, and I kayoed the horse with one punch between the eyes. Mel Brooks was present for that scene and he used it many years later in his film *Blazing Saddles*.

I had sense enough to know that I had to find some outlet to get rid of my aggression, this totally destructive behavior. I had no understanding of my real problems in those days. I was groping. I was like the doctor in the Coast Guard who knew only how to deal with the most obvious surface manifestations.

Ever since the Coast Guard, I had been a gun nut and had acquired a large collection of weapons. Beginning in 1953, I figured out a way of using them to get rid of a lot of my anger. I had a friend, Harry Radutzky, who owned the Joyva Halvah Company. I asked him if he could vacuum-pack the little halvah cans with water, instead of halvah. He said, "Sure," and whenever I had time off from the show, Radutzky and I and another friend named Milt Chasen would go up to Florence's uncle's place in the Catskills. We'd find an isolated spot against the side of a hill and put the water-filled halvah cans on tree branches all over the area. Then we'd back off and fire at the cans with .220 rifles. The ammunition was so fast and generated so much heat, that every time we hit a can, it would explode in a geyser of steam. On each trip, we fired hundreds of rounds.

It *did* siphon off a lot of the rage in me.

It wasn't enough.

In fact, the guns led me into further problems. One day, I was having a screaming argument with Florence in our apartment at 940 Park Avenue. In the midst of the fight, I found myself picking up a Luger. I suddenly stopped yelling and said to myself, "My God, a man is having a fight with his wife and he grabs a gun? What am I coming to?"

I said aloud to Florence, "You've been talking about a psychiatrist ever since Europe. Just tell me where I'm supposed to go."

She said, "His name is Sidney Margolin and his office is a block away. Why do you think I picked this apartment for us?"

Dr. Margolin was a nice man, and I went to him for five years.

But he wasn't enough, either.

# 14

## "Three Winning Combinations Are Better Than One"

For the most part, psychoanalysis has never been very successful in the treatment of alcoholism—not then, and not now. Especially when the alcoholic still is in a state of what is called "denial": Who, me? Maybe I drink a little too much, but I can handle it; it doesn't really affect me.

Dr. Margolin was a Freudian, and Freudian psychoanalysis was very popular in those days. It was the in thing to do. You took fifty minutes out of your life every day, and you rambled on about your mother and your sister and your father

133

and your brother, and the doctor kept saying "Hmmm," and when the fifty minutes were up, it was, "See you tomorrow."

Nearly everyone on our staff at "Your Show of Shows" was in analysis. We spent a lot of time comparing our experiences with our doctors, which led to many funny psychiatrist skits in the show. It was fun, but not very productive for me. What I needed was someone to question me, to challenge my "denial," to make me face up to how I was slowly destroying myself. What I needed was a teacher. Psychoanalysis doesn't do that. "You have to work it out yourself—not only intellectually but emotionally." Today there are newer forms of psychiatry that are more effective with the problems I had. Group therapy might have done wonders for me—allowing me to recognize myself in others, making me realize that I was not alone.

The only other drinker on the show was Tony Webster, one of our better writers. I probably *did* see something of myself in him and related to him, because once, when he told me he was in bad shape from booze and had to go to a hospital, I not only gave him the time off but also a raise. Tony was the smart one. He went into Alcoholics Anonymous and stopped drinking completely years and years ago. He wrote a successful Broadway play, *The Greatest Man Alive;* and from "Sergeant Bilko" (after he left me) to "Love Boat" (today), he has been one of the most proficient writers in television.

A.A. was out of the question for me. Despite the anonymity of the program, NBC was certain that word of my problem would leak out. That would not do for one of *their* stars. So my drinking became one of the best-kept secrets in New York, in the same way that Spencer Tracy's drinking became one of the best-kept secrets in Hollywood. I found out that NBC had gone to my personal physician at the time and had prescribed chloral hydrate for me, saying, "This guy is drinking too much. For God's sake, give him something to wean him off the booze." So that's how I got started on the chloral hydrate *and* the booze. When that didn't seem to be working, my internist switched me to sodium amytal. When I lied to the psychiatrist, Dr. Margolin, about not taking any drugs at all, *he* prescribed the tranquilizer Miltown "to help me sleep." With the Miltown, the sodium amytal, and the alcohol, all together, I slept pretty good.

But *still*—miraculously—my work on the show was not yet affected. Our fourth year on the air (the season of 1953–54) was our best. We now were doing satires of other successful TV series of the day, along with our movie and opera spoofs. The critics and the public loved our kidding of television itself. One of our classics—which was replayed as recently as 1982 in a TV tribute to Pat Weaver—was called "This Is Your Story." It was, of course, a put-on of "This Is Your Life."

Carl Reiner was the Ralph Edwards-like host of "This Is Your Story" and I was Al Duncey, a poor schnook sitting in the audience, waiting for someone else to have the intimacies of his life exposed to the public. Duncey himself is the one whose story is to be told that night.

This skit is a perfect example of how we improvised on the air in live television and frequently made things much funnier than they were written for the Wednesday night deadline. Here's the first page of the script.

*Open on set, Carl enters, carrying large, flowery and satin-covered book*

CARL: Welcome America, to "This Is Your Story." (*Starts into the audience*) As you know, every week on "This Is

Your Story," we show to the entire nation the intimate inside story of some person's life. (*Coyly*) And whose story do you think it will be tonight? (*Camera pans around audience*) Will it be your story, or will it be your story, or will it be *your* story?

*Camera zooms to Sid, sitting in audience. Sid looks to either side of him. Business of not believing it could be him.*

CARL: Yes, this is *your* story, Al Duncey!

SID (*More reaction to people around him*): Aw, he must be kiddin'. He's kiddin', ain't he? I mean, after all? He's kiddin', ain't he?

That isn't the way we did it on the air. When Carl names Al Duncey as the night's biographee, I say absolutely nothing. I look at the man next to me, who just happened to be an NBC bigwig named Dave Tebet, and I seem to take it for granted *he's* the chosen one and Carl made a mistake. When Carl approaches me with the big satin book, I *still* say nothing. But all my actions indicate that I don't *want* my story told. As Carl tries to lift me out of my seat, I fight him off. I hit him with my raincoat. I keep pushing him away.

Not a word of that is in the script, but it hilariously sets up the rest of the story—about a reluctant biographee who then proceeds to louse up Carl's entire "This Is Your Story" episode.

My silent but violent protest when Carl first approached me was infinitely funnier than my written dialogue: "Aw, he must be kiddin'" and so on; and the improvisation changed the entire thrust of the skit—for the better.

But sometimes the improvisations *didn't* work, and in live television, you couldn't go back and fix them. We had a

running routine, for example, about four stiff-upper-lip Brit-
ishers (Carl, Imogene, Howard, and me) who sat in a line in
four chairs and never were perturbed by anything—even when
they were pelted with water, and worse. Tony Webster came
up with the idea of doing "The British," as we called the
routine, with a chimpanzee clambering all over them—and,
as usual, they don't blink an eye. Their dignity remains intact.

We called in an animal trainer and his chimp on the day
of the show. The chimp was absolutely marvelous in rehearsal.
He jumped up and down on us, pulled our hair, played with
our neckties, even removed Imogene's shawl and wrapped
himself in it. It looked as if this was going to be one of the
funniest skits we had ever done.

We broke for dinner before air-time, and the animal trainer
made the mistake of giving the chimp *his* dinner, too.

At eight o'clock, we got our cue and we were on the network.
"The British" skit came up early in the show. The four of us
sat down in our line of chairs, and then the chimp was pushed
out onto the stage. The chimp did *nothing*. He was fed and
well satisfied and probably figured, "What the hell? Who
needs to perform now?" So he just sat there, in the same line
with the rest of us. He was as dignified and tight-lipped as
we were—which was funny for about five seconds—but what
was going to get the laughs after that?

Max had to order the curtain rung down and Carl and I
had to fill up the time later by ad-libbing a Professor sketch
we just barely had formulated in the back of our heads.

But there were more hits than misses, and as we approached
the end of the 1953–54 season, it looked as if "Your Show
of Shows" would be a fixture on NBC for at least another
decade.

We didn't figure on the corporate mind.

# Where Have I Been?

First, we began to hear rumors. The rumors, picked up and printed by the TV columnists, indicated that some NBC officials were wondering why so much talent should be used up in a single series. Why not break us up into three, four, or even five series, which would multiply the profits of the network?

The rumor became fact when Hal Janis came to see me one day in my dressing room. Hal, a sweet but always mournful-looking man, was an NBC executive who was the permanent liaison with our show. He eventually worried himself to death.

I said to Hal, "What about these rumors?"

He said, "They're true. There's a big shake-up coming."

I got a sinking feeling. "What kind of shake-up?"

He said, "They want to split you into three parts. Next season, you will do your own show with your own production company. Imogene will also do her own show. And Max is going to produce what he calls 'spectaculars.' We're going to give him our biggest sound stage in Brooklyn and turn him loose on all of those musical production numbers he loves so much. If he wants to do whole operettas like *The Desert Song*, we'll get him Nelson Eddy and even a hundred tons of sand from Coney Island. You can do mostly comedy on your show, and so can Imogene on her show."

Stunned, I asked, "But why break up a winning combination?"

Hal shrugged and said, "TV is like betting on the horses today, and like they say at the racetrack, three winning combinations are better than one."

We spent the last month of the season figuring out how we were going to split up the talent. Max took the choreographers and most of the musical people. Lucille Kallen, who had worked very well with Imogene, elected to go with her. To

138

my surprise so did Mel Brooks. I inherited Carl Reiner and Howard Morris, among the performers. Head writer Mel Tolkin split up with his old partner, Lucille, and came with me. Of the rest of the writing staff, I got Tony Webster and Neil and Danny Simon. It was all very amicable. There was a lot of hugging and crying and wishing each other good luck.

Financially, there was nothing to worry about. Earlier in "Your Show of Shows," NBC had given $1 million guaranteed contracts to both Imogene and me. If the worst happened, we'd each get one hundred thousand dollars a year from the network for ten years for doing nothing. Emotionally, however, I was a mess. I was going to be completely on my own, without Max, for the first time in years. I began to regret having fought with him whenever he cut one of our comedy numbers to give a little extra time to his musical numbers. But, at the same time, I was happy for Max because I knew he was a man ahead of his time, that this was his opportunity to do the most impressive productions television had ever seen. I would try my best to get along without him. I was cocky; I looked forward to being the complete and total boss. I was scared; I still wanted the hands on the carriage.

These ambivalent feelings got muted in the technical and financial preparations for what lay ahead. My lawyer, Milton Mound, set up my new production company. I named it Shellric, after my children Shelly and Rick (later I added a "k" when our third child, Karen, was born, and the company name became Shellrick). Then we rented several floors of the Milgrim Building on Fifty-seventh Street just off Fifth Avenue. This would be our production, writing, and rehearsal facility.

When all was ready, I had a big party for the staff and cast. I made a long pep-talk speech about our plans for what NBC wanted to call "Caesar's Hour."

## Where Have I Been?

In the middle of my speech, Tony Webster, who was smashed, yelled out, "Why don't you sit down, you big, fat bastard!"

Everybody laughed. Drunks are funny.

I laughed, too.

After all, *I* wasn't a drunk.

# 15

## "Will Trade You Larry Gelbart for Two Oil Wells"

NBC's gamble didn't pay off the way they would have liked. Imogene's show was well done but its ratings were not as good as expected and it was canceled in less than a year. Max did some marvelous and innovative things in his "spectaculars" (for example, he actually *did* do the entire *Desert Song* with Nelson Eddy and tons of sand). He paved the way for hundreds of big TV extravaganzas to come. Max's "spectaculars" were on the air irregularly, however, which made it difficult to build up a steady, loyal, week-after-week audience.

Only "Caesar's Hour" took off, in a big way. It was just

sixty minutes, compared with the hour and a half of "Your Show of Shows," but people didn't seem to notice the difference.

## Carl Reiner

*It annoys me today when people talk about the Golden Age of TV comedy and everything we did is labeled "Your Show of Shows." Hardly anybody realizes that there were two shows. There were four years of "Your Show of Shows," followed immediately in the same spot in the schedule by "Caesar's Hour," which was on for three more years.*

*Actually, the best work we did was in "Caesar's Hour." Granted, none of it would have happened if we hadn't perfected our techniques in "Your Show of Shows," but I get tired of reporters raving about some sketch "you did on 'Your Show of Shows' with Sid Caesar" when actually it was on "Caesar's Hour," maybe two years after "Your Show of Shows" had ceased to exist. I guess it's become sort of a generic term for our comedy of that particular period.*

This misinterpretation of the historical facts doesn't bother me as much as it seems to bug Carl. All I know is that "Caesar's Hour" held most of the old "Your Show of Shows" audience and our work *did* get better.

With the exception of the production numbers, everything *looked* the same. To the audience, the only visible change was that Nanette Fabray had replaced Imogene Coca. In our so-called "domestic sketches"—the husband-and-wife bits— we were now the Victors instead of the Hickenloopers. The only other difference was that Nanette is a fine singer and dancer, and we made more and more use of those talents of hers in various types of sketches.

I'm often asked if I missed Imogene. Of course I did. She's a great actress and we grew so used to working together onstage that she could guess what I was going to say—and react to it—when the thought still was in my head. Offstage, we were not that close. I'm basically a loner, and so is Imogene. We'd go to occasional parties at one another's houses. Apart from that, we did little socializing—not that *any* of us had much time for socializing with those crazy live-TV schedules and the six days a week of writing and rehearsing. Besides, Imogene became more and more withdrawn after her husband, Bob, died suddenly during the second year of "Your Show of Shows." Bob was an alcoholic.

I selected Nanette Fabray because I remembered how brilliant she had been as a guest star in one of our silent-movie satires on "Your Show of Shows." To me, our silent movies were the best test of a person's ability. If someone reacts and you can tell what she's saying—even without your being able to see the subtitles—then you know you can work with her in anything. It's basic instinct, no words, just looks.

In "Caesar's Hour," Nanette turned out to be everything I expected. She was totally different from Imogene; there's no way to compare them as actresses—but she was just as effective. As people, they're both wonderful, wonderful women. But, as in my relationship with Imogene, there was little or no socializing. I guess it mostly was my fault. By the time the socializing-hour came along, I generally was out of it.

Once again, I credit the success of the show to the writing. Writing is the beginning and end of everything, so I did whatever I had to do to keep getting the best. For example, I heard about a young kid who was writing for Bob Hope.

His name was Larry Gelbart. I liked what I knew about his background, which had a lot of similarities to mine. Larry's father was a barber, and as a teenager he used to hang around telling jokes to comics like Danny Thomas while his father was cutting their hair. Eventually Danny hired him and that's how Larry got his start as a comedy writer, ending up in Bob Hope's stable of writers for five years. Another thing that attracted me to Larry was that I heard he had played the saxophone in school.

My people put out feelers to Larry, and Hope found out about them. Bob sent me a telegram: "Will trade you Larry Gelbart for two oil wells." Larry eventually came with us, for several reasons, which he explained to me later. "First," he said, "I saw your airplane number in *Tars and Spars* and I guess I did it in high school as often as you did it in the Coast Guard. In the second place, I wanted to be with the one comedian who didn't come out of the movies and radio and was the pure television performer. I liked the idea that you were willing to try any suggestion, no matter how crazy and original it was. You also reminded me of Harry Ritz of the Ritz Brothers, who was my comedy idol when I was a kid. You have the same knack of using your eyes, your face, your body, for very funny exaggeration."

The public doesn't remember Harry Ritz too well, but all good comics do. I was very flattered and welcomed Larry Gelbart aboard.

We also got Shelly Keller, Selma Diamond, Aaron Rubin, and Gary Belkin (all of whom now are major writer-producers in television). Mel Brooks came back after Imogene's show folded. Later, my stand-in, Milt Kamen, arrived with a wispy little fellow and said, "I want you to meet the young Larry Gelbart." Larry said, "Wait a minute, *I* am the young Larry

Gelbart." But that's how we acquired the young Woody Allen. The biggest sleeper of all was Mike Stewart, whom we called "The Typist." That's because he could do more than a hundred words a minute on the typewriter and he had replaced Lucille Kallen's longhand in recording our ideas and lines in the writers' room. He didn't say very much but a lot of his concepts worked themselves into our scripts. A good thing, too. Next to Neil Simon, Mike Stewart went on to become the most successful playwright to emerge from our writers' room. Among the many Broadway hits he wrote were *Hello, Dolly,* and *Bye, Bye Birdie*.

The writers' room was crazier than it had been on "Your Show of Shows." Desks were burned, people's shoes were ripped off their feet and thrown out the window onto Fifty-seventh Street. Writers in disfavor were sent off to work in what was called the "Jock Room," a downstairs rehearsal hall dressing room, where male dancers changed their clothes and hung their jockstraps.

Our head writer, Mel Tolkin, liked what he called "good creative anger." Tolkin says, "Nearly all of us were in therapy and we often took out our anger in our script ideas. I realized later that we got a lot of laughs out of murders. In one Italian-movie satire, for example, Sid stabs his wife to death, and then, while he's mourning and carrying on, a shoeshine boy comes in to polish his shoes. Almost absentmindedly, Sid plunges the knife into the kid's back. Then, after he's arrested, Sid walks past the morgue attendants carrying off the bodies, and he also matter-of-factly knifes one of *them*. It was all done so preposterously that it wasn't offensive, but it gives you some idea of how we were venting our aggressions against each other—in our writing."

Mel Brooks continued to be the instigator of a lot of this

tumult. Once, he infuriated Larry Gelbart, who had fallen asleep in a chair, with his feet up on a desk. Mel rapped the soles of Larry's shoes, as if he were a cop rousting a sleeping bum in the park. That was one of the times a Mel Brooks moccasin got tossed out the window, forcing him to go out and buy a whole new pair in order to go home. Another story everyone remembers is when I put my hand on Mel's head and I said, "I own this." Mel slipped his hand inside my pocket, pulled out my wallet, and said, "I own *this*."

There was so much screaming and yelling in the writers' room that a shy, soft-spoken man didn't have a chance of getting his ideas across. Woody Allen and Neil Simon both solved this problem by latching on to someone with a very loud mouth as a transmitter of their ideas. Carl Reiner, for example, was Doc's spokesperson. Doc always sat next to Carl, and whenever I'd see him lean over and whisper something in Carl's ear, I'd say to myself, "Aha, Doc has an idea." Then Carl would get up and bellow, louder than anyone else, "Doc's got an idea." Still shouting, he would tell the idea. It was almost always a good one, and it would be recorded by the typewriter of that other great playwright-to-be, Mike Stewart.

Working with such a roomful of geniuses day after day was the most exhilarating time of my life. I was the sole boss. Mine always was the final word on every line and bit of business that went into the show. I even lost my fear of not having Max Liebman around to back me up and to edit me. As time went on, that became a problem. As I have since learned, *everybody* needs an editor—both in work and in life. For me . . . ?

There was nobody there to say no.

Sure, the writers kidded me about my excesses, but kidding

was as far as they went. If only someone had said, "Sid, you're wrong," or "Sid, you're destroying yourself." But they were too much in awe of me. It was my fault. That's the way I structured it. I was the spoiled child who now had all the toys, and by God, they were *mine.*

The only one who came close to speaking up was Larry Gelbart. I guess it was that part of his personality that helped him create the wonderful irreverence of the TV series "M-A-S-H" later on. Larry said to me, "Sid, there's only one word I can think of in connection with you. The word is 'gigantism.' Everything you have is the biggest. Your suits have the biggest shoulders, your cuff links look like Mount Rushmore, your kids are the biggest I've ever seen for their age, you've got the biggest dog, you eat the biggest steaks, you drink the biggest drinks, that blue and white Cadillac of yours reminds me of the Queen Mary." And yet, Larry then pumped me up by telling me I also had the biggest talent, and by giving me a Christmas present of a gold throne to sit in at the writers' meetings.

There was nobody to say no.

They even protected me from my own foolishness.

There was an incident I don't even remember because I was so zonked out, but as Carl Reiner tells it, it may have been as funny-sad as any of the humorous-poignant Chaplin-esque sketches we now were doing so successfully on the show.

## Carl Reiner

*It was a Wednesday night and we hadn't quite finished that week's script. Something fell apart and we had to do a whole* new movie satire in one day. I usually left for home at six o'clock, but I stayed on that night for a dinner meeting with Sid and the writers at the Blair House restaurant. It was one of the few times most of us had seen the after-working-hours Sid Caesar.

We had a big table in the restaurant and I was sitting right next to Sid. He said, "First we'll all have a drink, and then we'll eat, and then we'll work." I knew he was taking a strong sedative at the time called Placidyl.

The waiter came over to take our food orders. The last to order was Sid, at the head of the table. I heard Sid say, "I'll have some fish, filet of sole, broiled filet of sole—and some shoestring potatoes."

Then Sid just sat there, looking blank, and he slumped forward. His head fell into a bowl of coleslaw that was there on the table. We all laughed. We thought it was some kind of joke.

The waiter went away, and Sid never moved. I shook him. I said, "He's out." I never saw anyone fall asleep like that. I was worried that he'd drown in the coleslaw, but he was breathing OK.

Then came one of the funniest ad-lib situations where everybody in the restaurant seemed to be passing by that table. They recognized me and came over to say hello. They didn't recognize Sid because his head was down. I said, "We've got to do something comedically, as if we're rehearsing a skit, or this thing will be in all the papers tomorrow."

We started doing shtick. With six comedy writers sitting there, a lot of imagination went into play. They must have come up with about thirty routines, all based on a guy sitting with his head down on the table in a bowl of coleslaw. I don't remember who did what, but one of the writers stood over Sid's back with a steak knife in his hand and said, "So, Inspector, this undoubtedly is the murder weapon, which makes the waiter immediately one of the chief suspects." People passed by to say hello but moved away when they saw what seemed to be a rehearsal.

Another group of people came up to the table. One of our guys said, "Let us pray," and we all put our heads down on the table. Once again, the visitors didn't stay. Another shtick: We acted as if we were at a seance. I said, "Let us all hold hands and see if we can raise the table."

This went on for about forty-five minutes. We kept examining Sid to make sure he was breathing. We finished our meal, had dessert and coffee, and the waiter came over with the check. He knew what was going on, so he stood next to me with the check, in the same place where he had stood when he was taking Sid's order.

Suddenly Sid's head came up. He said to the waiter, "And shoestring potatoes." It was as if the forty-five-minute blackout had never happened, and he was picking up in the middle of ordering at the exact moment when he had passed out.

I swear it's true. If Doc Simon or Larry Gelbart had invented that scene for our show, nobody would have believed it.

# 16

## "Those Were the Days, My Friend; We Thought They'd Never End"[©]

Maybe Doc Simon was trying to tell me something. Not long after the Blair House incident, he proposed that we do a long spoof of a silent movie—the kind they made in the early 1900s—about an up-and-coming young man who falls into the clutches of the Demon Rum and then goes steadily downhill to oblivion.

That was our Chaplin period, so we all threw ourselves

into making this forty-three-minute playlet a gem—which it turned out to be. It got me on the cover of *Newsweek*.

We called it "A Drunk There Was." The printed subtitles were hilarious:

A DRUNK THERE WAS! (THE STORY OF A FATHER'S FAILURE)

THE FATHER . . . TORN BETWEEN TWO GREAT LOVES, SCOTCH AND RYE.

THE MOTHER . . . WHO DIDN'T ORDER A MARRIAGE ON THE ROCKS.

THE BOSS . . . A FRIEND OF THE FAMILY AND AN ENEMY OF THE BOTTLE.

THE DRUNKARD'S DAUGHTER . . . DAUGHTER OF THE DRUNK-ARD.

THE DAUGHTER'S SUITOR . . . ALL DOORS WERE OPEN TO HIM BECAUSE HE WAS A HIGH SCHOOL GRADUATE.

THE VILLAIN . . . DEMON RUM.

I played Randolph, the father. Nanette Fabray was in the dual role of both my wife and my daughter. My boss was Howard Morris. Carl Reiner was the prized suitor with the high school diploma.

The movie opens in a happy home scene in which I am celebrating many things with my wife, Alice. It is her birthday and it is my birthday. It is our wedding anniversary. I have gotten a raise at work and I will now earn six dollars a week, with overtime. The canary has laid eggs. The cat has had kittens. And Alice is going to have a baby.

The boss comes in and proposes a toast: "I hope they'll all be boys." I resist the booze and the boss says, "Oh, just take one shot." The next subtitles:

LITTLE DID HE KNOW THAT THIS WOULD BE THE SHOT HEARD ROUND THE WORLD.

FIVE YEARS AND 6,522 BOTTLES LATER!

I am now guzzling booze hidden all around the office—in an inkwell, a table leg, a typewriter roller, even in the hollow center of a hat-rack. The boss comes in and fires me.

LIPS THAT HAVE TOUCHED LIQUOR SHALL NEVER LICK MY COM-PANY'S STAMPS.

I go steadily downhill. My wife, Alice, "joins the angels." My daughter grows up. For her sake, I stop drinking, but I can't shake my image as a reformed drunkard, who's "always afraid of John Barleycorn." My daughter falls in love with Rodney, the high school graduate. But . . .
Subtitle:

WHEN RODNEY FINDS OUT, HE WILL REFUSE TO MARRY A GIRL WHO BEARS A DRUNKARD'S NAME.

I ask my boss to adopt my daughter.

WITH YOUR GOOD NAME SHE CAN MARRY RODNEY, THE HIGH SCHOOL GRADUATE.

I make her hate me, and she is adopted by my boss, Mr. Edgewater.

NEWSPAPER HEADLINE: SOCIETY WEDDING TODAY. ALICE EDGEWATER TO MARRY RODNEY FORBES, THE HIGH SCHOOL GRADUATE.

With tears streaming from my eyes, I stand in the snow outside the Edgewater mansion, watching the wedding of my daughter through the window.

That final scene broke me up because I based it on the time my mother stood in the snow watching me come out of the Waldorf-Astoria. But in the euphoria of the entire country talking about the skit that week, I soon forgot all my personal identifications with it.

Another classic of that period began as Larry Gelbart's idea. We did a movie satire called "Aggravation Boulevard," which again combined the humor and pathos of the Charlie Chaplin-Buster Keaton tradition. The skit was based on the story of John Gilbert, who had been a huge silent-film star but who was ruined when talking movies came in and the public learned he had a high squeaky voice. In keeping with our particular brand of satire, we took it just one half-note further. As our hero, Mr. Rex Handsome, *my* voice turned out to be a rather effeminate pure soprano, which made it even more ludicrous when I played a gunfighter scene, for instance, walking into an Old West bar, shooting a bad guy, and then asking tremulously, "Who else is looking for trouble?"

It was funny-sad, even pathetic, as I sat by the phone waiting for producers to call, while my movie-star wife, Nanette, kept working, and my butler, Howard Morris, faked calls from studios requesting my services, which I then could indignantly turn down. I blamed it all on my director, Carl Reiner, who had had me wear "those crazy bloomers" in my last silent film, a Rudolph Valentino-like desert epic.

Unlike "A Drunk There Was," there was a very funny happy ending. It was discovered that when I caught a cold, my voice changed to a masculine basso profundo. So I would go through life, my stardom restored, by having water poured on me to keep a perpetual cold in effect.

People marvel today at how we were able to do an entire play like this *live* and make it look like a polished movie on the TV screen at home. It took a lot of improvising. For example, for audience scenes at the Hollywood premiere of Rex Handsome's first talking picture, we turned the cameras around and photographed our *own* audience in the Century Theater.

On the stage, which extended over part of the audience area, we had sets of the interior of Rex Handsome's home, the interior of producer Flo Florenz's office, and the interiors of two movie sound stages on which two different Rex Handsome movies were being filmed (one a desert epic, the other a Western). As our plot progressed, we simply moved our cameras and ourselves from one set to the other. There was no time for mistakes. Exterior shots—say the outside of producer Florenz's Vita Cash Studios—were accomplished by training one camera on photographs. The passage of time was indicated by flipping cards (imprinted with days and years) in front of the same camera.

The scripts, of course, no longer are available—not even to film schools and universities—but let me share with you a couple of scenes from my own copies to indicate how such great playwrights-to-be as Neil Simon, Larry Gelbart, and Joe Stein managed to accomplish so much with so little.

The first is the terribly poignant scene after Rex Handsome's squeaky voice is heard by a movie audience for the first time and is laughed out of the theater:

*Calendar shows Monday, Tuesday, Wednesday, Thursday, Friday, Saturday, Sunday . . . January, February, March, April, May, June, July . . . 1929, 1930, 1931 . . . Sid is still sitting at the telephone in his library, where we left him in the last scene. . . . Howie comes up to him.*

HOWIE: Sir, you've been waiting by that phone for four years. At least have something to eat.

SID: No . . . The phone may ring at any minute and I don't want to have food in my mouth.

HOWIE: Maybe they forgot your number, sir.

SID: How could they forget Crestview 1? I was the first person in the whole world to get a telephone.

*Howie crosses to Nanette.*

HOWIE: Begging your pardon, madame, but I'd like a word with you.

NANETTE: What is it, Rutherford?

HOWIE: Well, frankly, madame, he's flipped his stack. Why just yesterday, he made me call him on the extension phone and offer him a job . . . and he turned me down. That's the state we're in. So you see how it is with us, madame.

*We see Howie as a bit flipped himself.*

SID: Rutherford . . . call me and offer me a starring part in a big naval picture with Lana Turner.

HOWIE: Here we go again.

NANETTE: That settles it then. I've got to go to the studio and see Mr. Florenz myself.

Our cameras moved about ten feet, and in the very next scene, the at-home audience saw Nanette bursting into the set depicting Carl's lavish office at Vita Cash Studios. Two scenes later, with another short camera move across the stage, they were looking into an authentic Old West saloon, as producer Florenz gave Rex Handsome his second shot at starring in a talking movie:

CARL: Lights . . . camera . . . sound.

*We go to the western set. A barroom. Two guys.*

SHERIFF (*to Milt*): He's coming here to kill you. I can't protect you. You killed his brother and now he's coming for revenge.

MILT: I'll take care of him when he gets here.

SHERIFF: But you don't understand. He's changed. He's turned into a killer. Here he comes now.

*Footsteps outside . . . doors swing open*

MILT: Draw!

*Two shots ring out. One guy comes up, tries to take gun out of his hand. Sid jiujitsus him and knocks him down.*

SID (*in his high effeminate voice*): Anybody else looking for trouble? For once and for all, there's going to be law and order in this town . . . and I'm going to see to it!

*Two guys snicker. One nudges the other guy. Quick pan down to Sid. He looks up . . . slowly . . . then drops the guns, and slowly walks off the set.*

HOWIE: I'll get the car, sir.

NANETTE: Rex . . . It's just a mistake. It's just a mistake. They didn't mean it.

*He pushes her aside and walks off. Nanette runs to the center of the set.*

NANETTE: . . . How dare you! How dare you laugh at him. That was Rex Handsome. You worked with him for fifteen years . . . and now, now you laugh at him. Shame on you. Shame on all of you. Shame on Hollywood. No wonder the biggest street in Hollywood is named Aggravation Boulevard.

*Carl comes up to Nanette*

CARL: I'm sorry, Mara, I really am. I gave everyone orders not to laugh. . . . But let's face it, he has a funny voice.

That's when I come back, wringing wet from having been caught in the rain, and with a deep basso profundo voice because of having caught a cold. The skit rushes on to its climax. In thirty-three minutes, we have accomplished the near-impossible—with seven scene changes and a dozen costume changes. And all without leaving the stage of the Century Theater for all of those thirty-three *live* minutes.

Again the critics raved. With our roomful of writing geniuses, it seemed that everything we touched turned to gold. Even our inevitable live-television goofs turned out for the better.

When we were on the air one night, we had an accident

backstage. A chunk of scenery fell on Nanette and she had to be rushed to the hospital. Fortunately, it turned out that she was just bruised, but in the meantime, I was stuck onstage with about five minutes to fill before the end of the show. I was in my "Professor" costume, with my battered high hat, grungy tailcoat, and tie askew. I decided to make the know-it-all professor a musical expert. I went into the orchestra pit to guide the musicians in tuning up their instruments. The Professor, of course, loused everything up as he went from the string section, to the woodwinds, to the percussionists. It was a very successful five-minute ad-lib.

Another time, I was playing a great defense attorney, much like Clarence Darrow, in a courtroom drama. I delivered an impassioned summation to the jury about the innocence of my client, Howard Morris, and the extra who played the jury foreman got so carried away by my speech that he said "not guilty," when the verdict was supposed to be guilty. His goof was about to ruin the entire skit, so I said, "What do you mean 'not guilty'? This little rat is *not guilty?*" I then had to ad-lib an entire new speech to the jury to convince them that my client, Howard, really did deserve the electric chair. Clarence Darrow must have been turning over in his grave, but the skit turned out funnier than it had been written—and the audience and the critics never knew the difference.

As the song went, "Those were the days, my friend; we thought they'd never end."©

Nearly everything worked—even when we started out with a misguided premise. For example, many of us had musical backgrounds (Larry and I played the saxophone, Mel Tolkin played the piano, Mike Stewart wrote special material for stage musicals), and we would frequently spend an evening at the pop-music hangout Birdland to keep up with the latest trends. It was the time of spaced-out progressive jazz, so we did our usual slight exaggeration and came up with a new running character for the show, Cool Seas. As I played him, getting back to the saxophone after all those years, he spoke gibberish and wore thick glasses that looked like the bottoms of Coke bottles.

The first time I did Cool Seas on the air, I got a letter from a teacher somewhere in the Midwest. She said she worked with children who had poor sight, all of whom loved my show, and that it hurt them that I was making fun of people who had to wear powerful eyeglasses in order to see. That letter devastated me. I've always had a thing about failing or defective sight. When I was in school in Yonkers, I appointed myself protector of one little kid who was cross-eyed. Most of my fights in junior high were with guys who tried to pick on this boy.

So I got off a letter of apology to the teacher, assuring her that we'd change the character. And we did. Our be-bop musician now became Progress Hornsby. He was exactly the same as Cool Seas, except that he didn't wear glasses. Progress Hornsby became just as much of a favorite with the public— maybe even more so.

This was the time, too, of the enormous surge of rock music, with one barely-known group after another appearing on "The Ed Sullivan Show" on Sunday nights. We could not let this phenomenon escape our satire. So we got crazy-looking slicked-down wigs, and Carl, Howard, and I became the Haircuts. The Haircuts were a running feature on the show in 1956 and 1957. It was exciting for us because there was very little writing, just a lot of ad-libbed insanity.

It was impossible to understand the lyrics of the songs we were singing. They were out-of-tune and out of synchronization.

159

Occasionally, you could hear an exaggerated "I lo-o-o-o-ove you" or a "baby-baby-baby," in the style of the day. Funniest of all were our movements as we sang our nonsense. We never stood still. We ran up and down the stage, frequently with our backs to the audience. We waved our arms, snapped our fingers, gyrated our pelvises—but never in time with one another. My behind, which was quite large at the time, was the klutziest of all as I did my bumps and grinds. It was disorganized chaos on the stage, but like all of our best material, it was not too far from the real thing—so people could look at it, recognize it, and laugh—even the kids who went to genuine rock concerts and watched "The Ed Sullivan Show" faithfully for their musical heroes.

Yes, those were the days. Even my personal life seemed to have leveled off. Florence found a big beautiful house for us overlooking Long Island Sound at King's Point in Great Neck, New York, and we moved to the suburbs from Park Avenue. We had acres of hilly, wooded property. The novelty of it gave me a natural high. I even slowed down periodically on the booze and the pills, as I sat on our land, or on the boat we bought, looking over the peaceful seascape.

In 1956 Karen, our third and last child, was born. I still wasn't much of a father, but Florence was acting as both mother *and* father to the kids—holding the family together. She was so busy with PTA and car-pooling and even going to father-son functions with Rick, that I was able to fool her for quite some time. Or so I thought. With my Placidyl, which my internist kept prescribing as if it were aspirin, at least I was quiet and not abusive to her at home. When I'd fall asleep in my chair at night after loading up with Placidyl and Scotch in my limousine on the long ride home, I thought she believed this was just the natural result of working so hard on such a successful show.

But as I know now, I wasn't fooling her at all. It was the placidity caused by the Placidyl that made me easier to contend with.

When the unraveling began in 1958, the Placidyl didn't help. Nothing did.

# 17
# The Unraveling

After two such great years for "Caesar's Hour," it was hard to believe so many things could go wrong at once. First, we lost Nanette at the beginning of the 1957–58 season. It was one of those unfortunate circumstances where her lawyers demanded much more money for her, and my lawyers said we couldn't afford it—and she left. We replaced her with Janet Blair, who was very good. Nanette had built up quite a following, however, and we seemed to have lost some of our rhythm and cohesion. It wasn't true, because Janet was very talented in a different kind of way, but that's the way the public perceived it.

The rhythm factor was very important because the television industry was in a state of turmoil then. Pat Weaver had been replaced at NBC by Robert Sarnoff (General David Sarnoff's son) and Robert Kintner. Taped shows—the "new technology" of the day—were coming in and both Sarnoff and Kintner were excited about being able to edit the tape and thus get what they thought would be sterilized perfection on the air. In preparation for this supposed millennium, there was a lot of shifting around and experimentation with the scheduling of the live shows.

The year before, for example, we had lost one of our Saturday nights every month to a show called "The Colgate Comedy Hour." Thus, we were on three weeks out of four. "The Colgate Comedy Hour" was different every month, with hosts like Danny Thomas, Jimmy Durante, and Martin and Lewis. The show was nothing like ours. It depended on the star personalities of its various hosts, with stand-up comedy monologues, production numbers, and sketches that largely had been developed for other media, such as vaudeville, nightclubs, and films. *Our* loyal audience would tune in and wonder where we were.

It didn't hurt us at first. But by 1958 the eight-year American habit of watching us *every* Saturday night was declining. Maybe the break in continuity had something to do with it—the loss of Imogene followed by the loss of the equally appealing Nanette—but our ratings began to slide for the first time. Not seriously. After all, we *did* still have all that great talent in the writers' room. Nonetheless, the handwriting was on the wall. A loss of a couple of more ratings points and Sarnoff and Kintner moved us to Monday night. There, we came up against two juggernauts representing the *new* fads: "The Arthur Godfrey Show" and "The Lawrence Welk Show."

In the meantime, I also suffered a setback in my personal life. Dr. Margolin, my psychoanalyst, closed his practice in

New York and moved to Denver. I didn't think I'd be so affected by his leaving me. He hadn't done me much good with my basic problems of booze and pills, but at least he had kept me on somewhat of an even keel emotionally. He was a crutch—not a very effective crutch, but aside from Florence, he was the only crutch I had. I went into a panic.

Dr. Margolin tried to counter my anxiety by turning me over to Dr. Lawrence Kubie, a famous psychoanalyst of that period, who was very well known for a best-seller book he had written on the subject of neurosis. He was a big man in literary circles, from which he derived many of his patients.

I began my sessions with Dr. Kubie in December 1957. He said to me, "Why are you here?"

I said, "Well, I'd like to stop drinking, if I can."

He said, "You stop drinking by stopping drinking."

I said, "I'm aware of that. The thought has occurred to me."

He said, "Well, the Christmas holidays are coming up. You will have no drinks. Nothing."

I said, "Wait a minute. I'm going to have to go to NBC parties. I'm going to have to go to sponsors' parties. . . ."

He said, in his heavy German accent: "You will drink nothing." I thought at the time that it was like the Gestapo talking.

I said, "I'll give it a try."

He said, "You won't give it a try. You'll *do*."

So I went through the Christmas holidays and I had a total of three drinks, which was like *nothing*, compared with what I had been doing for years.

When I came back for my next session with Kubie, I said, "Well, I only had three drinks in all this time. . . ."

I was about to continue when he flicked on his intercom

to his secretary. He said, "Case of S.C. will be closed and the file put away. Mark it 'incorrigible.' " Then, turning to me, "You are dismissed, Mr. Caesar."

I said, "You didn't look at your watch, Kubie. You see, I've got forty minutes left on this fifty-minute hour, and you're going to sit here and listen to me. You know, Kubie, I never talked about you as a gimp, because I didn't want to make you aware that you're a gimp, a cripple, a nothing, and a man who's got no sensitivity, he's got no time. You've only got time for books—all that crap you're putting out to the public. . . ."

I went on like that for the forty minutes. At one point, he said, "You get out of here."

I said, "Are *you* going to throw me out? Are you going to call a cop? I'll bury you in the chair there."

I was really very hostile. It was not one of my finer moments. Finally, I looked at my watch and said, "Well, the forty minutes are up. Go, Kubie. Go count your money." And I left.

The sad thing about it is that he was right. If I had only known then what I know now: that the only way you stop drinking is by stopping drinking. If he had only tried to get it across to me with less authoritarianism, more sensitivity. If I had only been less aggressive and willing to accept the idea. . . . But I know now that the word "if" should be cut out of the English language.

In any event, I was not in very good shape when "Caesar's Hour" continued into the second half of the season, the winter and spring of 1958.

I didn't realize it until I later saw the kinescopes of the shows we did then, but a scary thing was happening. For the first time in my life, the booze and pills were overlapping into my working days. I had always prided myself on the fact that no matter how much alcohol and sedative I took after hours, I'd always be able to shake off the effects by the next morning. Now, apparently, my big strong body wasn't metabolizing the stuff so efficiently anymore.

I looked at the kinescopes after the shows had been on the air, and I realized I wasn't coordinating. My timing was off. I was repeating myself, figuring that if I didn't make a point, the audience wouldn't get it. I forgot that I already had made the point, so I made it again. As a result, our sketches were running too long.

Hindsight is beautiful. But when you're young and you're scared and you run, you don't know where to lie down. You should say, "That's it. You've got to go to the hospital and get cleaned up, and start afresh." Instead of doing that, you keep trying to meet the pressures and you're destroying yourself.

I kept trying, and I was destroyed. One day in April 1958 I got a call from Robert Kintner at NBC, saying that he wanted to see me. He came over to the Century Theater on Fifty-ninth Street, where we did the show. He had Bob Sarnoff with him, also an NBC lawyer. I thought they wanted to talk about plans for "Caesar's Hour" for the next season. We were still doing well, even in the face of my problems, our Monday night competition, and the onrushing tide of new taped shows. I was so confident we would be renewed that I was in the process of trying to buy the entire Milgrim Building, which housed our production headquarters on the penthouse floors.

Kintner said, "Sid, we're going to cancel you." That was it. No "I'm sorry." No "Thank you for eight good years." No nothing. Kintner said, "About that million-dollar guarantee you have with us for one hundred thousand dollars a year . . ." I was in total shock, but I was about to cut in and say, "You can take your million-dollar guarantee and shove it up your ass." Instead, I went over to the side of the room with my lawyer, Richard Wincor.

"What does that guarantee mean?" I asked.

Wincor said, "It means they have to keep paying you, but you're exclusive to NBC for ten years if you ever do anything in television. My advice is to tell them you want to abrogate the deal. Ten minutes after this news gets out, the other networks will be after you."

So I went back over to Kintner and his group and told them I didn't want the guarantee. They didn't put up any kind of a fight. In fact, they looked relieved. Their attitude was that they weren't too anxious to hold on to me. I knew what they were saying to themselves: "He's a drunk. He won't accept help. Let's dump him." They left. It was done. That was the way it was supposed to be done.

It's funny, the things you think of at times like that. I thought of Judy Garland. I always had a certain empathy for her and she for me. Whenever we were in the same town, we'd always go to see each other work. One time she showed up in a nightclub where I was appearing. She was a mess and had lipstick smeared all over her face and her dress. She had a couple of young guys with her. I grabbed them and I said, "For God's sake, why don't you take care of her?"

Then I said to Judy, "Please, please, try to pull yourself together. Look what you're doing." I remembered how embarrassing it was for me to say that to her. I was doing the same thing.

The despair didn't hit me until I was on my way home from that meeting with Kintner and the other NBC people. Suddenly, all the things I had been afraid of for years had come to pass.

I was the tiny infant in the carriage looking up in panic to realize there were no loving hands on the carriage anymore, to keep me from rolling down the hill.

I was the young man watching the deterioration of my father and his financial ruin—and then there was my certainty that it was a prediction of what was going to happen to me.

I was the star, suffering unbearable guilt because a boy is not supposed to surpass his father in life.

There was the unbearable guilt of watching my mother in the snow across the street from the Waldorf-Astoria.

I was being punished.

And the one who was doing the punishing of Sid Caesar was—and would be, for many years to come now—Sid Caesar.

# 18

# "It Was All One Big Black Blob"

Depression. It rolled over me like a poisoned fog.

When I was informed of the cancellation of "Caesar's Hour," we still had four shows to do to finish out the season. I had to go into that writers' room and get up on the stage of the Century Theater, to try to put *something* together. Today, when a show is dropped, the remaining segments already are in the can. The network engineers merely unspool already produced film or tape. With us, being "live," there was nothing. The writers and Carl and Howard were just as numb as I was. The creative juices in us had totally evaporated. We'd just sit there looking at one another until someone would say, "Let's repeat such-and-such a monologue" or "Let's redo such-and-such a sketch." It was like a wake, trying to pick over the past accomplishments of the dead.

Somehow we managed to get through it. When it was over, I went home to the palliative of my pills and booze. Even though I was not working, I maintained a strange ethic about it. The pills were for the daytime; I'd still hold off on the booze until night. Florence would throw the prescriptions and alcohol down the toilet, but I'd always manage to get more. One of my most devastating experiences of that period was when my son Rick, then only seven, took all my whiskey bottles and hid them from me in his room. His older sister, Shelly, eleven, found them and said, "My God, my brother's an alcoholic, too." The shock of that made me quit everything for a few days, but it didn't last. What did an eleven-year-old kid know? I was not an alcoholic or an addict. I was just in the process of punishing myself. Part of the punishment was to induce sleep.

Which was death.

Why, in my mind, did I have to punish myself? In addition to the guilt I felt about my father and mother, I was convinced the time had now come to pay for all the good things that had happened to me. It was like when my mother put the food on my plate and it all had to come out even. The rewards of twelve years of constant success—from *Tars and Spars* to "Caesar's Hour"—now had to be evened up with pain and retribution. That's because I never really understood why I had my talent, and I believed I didn't deserve the unbroken string of successes that had come to me. I really believed that some Power was responsible for what I had been able to do, and I was the instrument through which the Power worked.

I myself was nothing. I was not responsible for all those good things that had happened. I was just lucky. I didn't realize then that you make your own luck. So the way I reasoned it out in my depression, part of me had accepted the gifts of the Power, and another part of me had responded badly and ungratefully to the Power. The Power was angry. The bad part of me had thought I was having great times— being drunk and stoned, never knowing about what I had done, having to be told the next day whom I had insulted. The Power now had decided I should be handcuffed to myself, to suffer, to pay for what I had done. I couldn't face this type of retribution, so my only answer was the easiest way out— to seek more oblivion in booze and pills.

It was all one big black blob. The Internal Revenue Service came after me. They were disallowing all the deductions I had taken for my company. "A television actor just gets up on a stage and acts, so why did you need your own office and staff? A television actor can drive and take taxis just like anyone else, so why did you need a limousine and chauffeur? Why did all the members of your staff charge all their meals to your company? Why did you pay your lawyer an eighty-thousand-dollar-a-year retainer? Why did you deduct so much for tips on your entertainment expenses?" And so on, and so on, and so on.

Such deductions are routinely accepted by the IRS today, but mine was one of the first of the independent television production companies, and such a deviation from the routine was not yet understood by the bureaucratic mind. My accountant gave in to the IRS—perhaps a bit too easily—and I was hit with hundreds of thousands of dollars in back payments and fines. The same accountant later represented Ronald Reagan, with much happier results for the president-to-be. I just went along with *my* settlement. I deserved it. It was part of my punishment, which had started the very day I had come home from being canceled. I had looked out my bedroom window and had seen people, invited by Florence, having a pleasant party around our swimming pool. I had stared at them and thought of my father's bankruptcy, and said to myself, "Christ, I can't afford even this anymore."

Florence was the strong one. Even through the IRS mess, she kept herself in control. She tried to reason with me—"We've still got enough money; there's plenty of work for you out there"—and she got me to go back to the new psychiatrist I had acquired after the Dr. Kubie fiasco.

His name was Dr. Sidney Carr, and he did me some good. He was the only psychiatrist who ever talked to me. Also, miraculously, he never charged me a cent, saying, "Part of your problem is that you seem to resent having to pay for therapy." He convinced me that a numbness I had developed in my legs came from too much alcohol, and I even let up on the booze—for a while. I was so carried away by the slight improvement I felt with Dr. Carr that I did an interview with *Look* magazine about the wonders of modern-day psychoanalysis. My enthusiasm was a little premature.

I kept waiting for the other networks to call—the way my lawyer had said they would when I was dropped by NBC. I began to feel like the silent-movie star, Rex Handsome, in my skit "Aggravation Boulevard," sitting by the telephone. Finally, there *was* a call. Not from CBS or ABC but from the BBC in London. The British were just getting into television broadcasting in a big way. The BBC wanted me for a thirteen-week half-hour series. Once again, Florence was the strong one. She said, "Let's go. It's better than your just sitting around the house."

So we flew to England and I did the show. It wasn't very good. The sets and the sound stages were rudimentary. It was like doing television in King Arthur's Court, with stone floors, stone sets, stone furniture. Nothing could be moved. I was rudimentary, too. I wasn't capable of doing anything but going through the motions, drawing on my instincts and my old material. I didn't make any effort to understand the British type of music-hall humor, and I'm sure a lot of my material made no sense to the British. I was creamed by the critics.

But a couple of interesting things happened. First of all, there *was* one solitary publication that liked me enormously. That was the famous, sophisticated English humor magazine *Punch*, which stated, "A real talent is here." As recently as February 1982, *Punch*'s editor, Alan Coren, wrote that when Johnny Carson's "Tonight Show" came to British TV with unfortunate results, "Mr. Carson had been heavily premarketed to us . . . as some extraordinary amalgam of Sid Caesar and Gore Vidal."

The second thing that happened during my thirteen bad weeks on the BBC—perhaps related to my review in *Punch*—was that a lot of young British comedians became aware of my different style of comedy. Among them were Dudley Moore, Peter Cook, and the people who later made up the marvelous Monty Python group. Peter Cook recently said that they all were influenced by me and by what they eventually saw in kinescopes of "Your Show of Shows" and "Caesar's Hour" smuggled into the country by British Overseas Airways pilots.

So my stint on the BBC cannot be considered a total loss. I'm proud that such brilliant talents acknowledge that I sowed a few seeds among them.

The English trip did me some good at home, too. I guess I proved to the networks that I could still work. Although the public never knew about my addiction problems, the world of TV executives was like a small town, and the word had spread quickly. Now, however, CBS was willing to take a chance with me—not with another series, but with some scattered specials sponsored by the United States Steel Company. Specials still were not very expensive in those days, and if I fell apart, it would not entail too much of a financial loss.

Once again, I was not totally with it when I did these one-hour specials. Most of the time I was in that poison fog of depression, continuing to believe that I had to keep punishing myself. Occasionally, however, the fog would lift and there would be brief bright patches. For example, the creative juices flowed and the old excitement returned when I worked again in a writers' room with Larry Gelbart and Woody Allen. But then the special would be taped, and over, and the fog would roll back in again.

I did one of those specials with Art Carney and Shirley MacLaine. It was a strange experience. Art knew I was a drunk, and I knew he was a drunk, and we had kind of psychedelic conversations in which we tap-danced all around the subject. Once again. How sad that we couldn't come to grips with our problem, openly discuss it, exchange inner feelings, let the other know that he was not alone—the way people do today in group therapy programs. It was not yet the time. For me, the time was still twenty years off. For Art, it came sooner.

But we came up with a very funny show, which won the Sylvania Award that year. Art and I did a sketch in which he was an advertising man trying to instruct a politician who had never been on television before. I was the politician, doing everything wrong in spite of his advice, and nearly getting electrocuted by the camera cables in the process.

Then there was another good sketch about teenagers trying to enjoy themselves at a Dick Clark-type afternoon dance show on television. Art was Dick Clark, and hilarious. Shirley MacLaine and I were the teenagers. It was exciting working with her, an exhilarating throwback to the old days. Like Imogene Coca, she had the knack of responding to my thoughts before I even said them; like Nanette Fabray, she could express emotions brilliantly with both her face and her body.

Shirley inspired me to ad-lib and improvise for the first time since the best months of "Caesar's Hour." I came up with all sorts of ridiculous teenage slang of that era, and she would respond in kind. When I'd do that in rehearsals, she'd clap her hands in delight and say, "Where are you coming from?" It was the first time I had ever heard that expression. She used it and nearly went to pieces laughing, when, at the end of the skit, she asked me, "What are you going to do when you get out of school?" and I answered, "Anything that don't muss my hair."

We also did a takeoff on "Playhouse 90," which we called "Hothouse 90." It had occurred to me that the credits on those dramatic shows of the Golden Age were getting ridiculous, and we came up with a tongue-twisting routine about who was going to be the host, the co-host, the co-co-host, the star, the costar, and that "if you let me co-host this week, I'll let you be the star and co-co-host next week."

Once again, Shirley asked, "Where are you coming from?"

I wish I could have been able to give her a detailed and truly analytical answer.

# 19

## "There Were Brief Patches of Brightness in the Fog"

I guess there were enough flashes of the old Caesar to cause a revival of interest in me in 1960 and 1961.

But it was too much. And it all came at once.

Part of the overload was my fault. Because of my fears, I only wanted to make money; I thought money was the answer to everything. Part of it was the fault of my agent, William Morris, which, like all agents, lives on the commissions derived from its clients' work—and does not take body counts.

The first thing that happened was that Neil Simon called. Doc, after finishing up with "Caesar's Hour," had gone back to his favorite milieu to become one of the theater's outstanding young playwrights. He already had a big hit play running on Broadway, *Come Blow Your Horn.* When he phoned, he said that he had another stage project in mind and asked if I would meet him at his lawyer's office. I got "clean" for the meeting and went to see him.

Doc greeted me warmly and we talked about the old days on "Your Show of Shows" and "Caesar's Hour." They already were the "old days," though only five years had passed since we first met and got to be colleagues and friends.

Then Doc said, "I've acquired this book, *Little Me,* by Patrick Dennis and I'm going to write it as a play with music for Broadway. It's about a girl and the seven men in her life, over a period of time. I want one actor to play all seven men."

I said, "And that's why you called me here today?"

He said, "You've guessed."

I said, "*Me?* Playing *seven* guys?"

He said, "You're the only one I know who has the physical strength to do it."

I said, "I'm not so strong anymore."

He said, "Bullshit. You've lost a lot of weight, but you still look like a *shtarker* to me. Besides, it's not much tougher than what you did on 'Your Show of Shows.' I used to watch you play four or five characters a night, with those quick costume changes just offstage between skits. Amazing. That's basically the same as what you'll be doing in this play for me."

One of those brief patches of brightness in the fog.

We made the deal. Doc went home to write. There would be a final script and the beginning of rehearsals in a few months.

Then came a call from Stanley Kramer, the movie producer.

177

He said, "I'm doing a crazy picture with a crazy title, *It's a Mad, Mad, Mad, Mad World.* It's a spoof of those old-fashioned comedies where there's a crime committed and then everybody tries to double-cross everyone else."

I said, "Sounds interesting. Who's in it?"

Kramer said, "I expect to have Spencer Tracy, Milton Berle, Mickey Rooney, Jimmy Durante, Edie Adams, Dick Shawn, Phil Silvers, Buddy Hackett, Jonathan Winters, Terry-Thomas, Ethel Merman. . . ." He kept reeling off the names.

I said, "Hold it. And you want *me?*"

He said, "Well, it's a small part, but so is almost everybody's."

I said, "I'll take it. When do you want me in Los Angeles?"

He said, "Next week."

Which was fine. I'd do the picture and finish just in time to start rehearsals for *Little Me* in New York in the fall. Except that I didn't count on what the William Morris Agency was up to. They had also lined me up for a half-hour TV series on ABC in the fall. It was to be called "As Caesar Sees It" and would reunite me with Carl Reiner, Imogene Coca, and Howard Morris—with Helena Rubinstein cosmetics as the sponsor.

I said to my agents: "How can I do three things at once?"

They said, "You'll manage. You should be glad. You haven't been that much in demand lately."

Instead of being glad, I was scared. I had just come through a period in which I had convinced myself, "They finally found me out. I'm not worthy. They're right." And now I had to face *them* again—on three fronts at once—without knowing whether the Power would relent and once again give me the talent to do it.

Being scared was dangerous for me. I went to see Dr. Carr.

I asked him for the hundredth time, "Why do I drink?" He said, for the hundredth time, "Your drinking and pill-taking are just symptoms. There are whole offshoots of your life that are destructive." He must have known that he was nearing the end of the line with me, so he went into more detail. "Your self-punishment," he said, "is more than just drinking. You will not let yourself be happy. You get yourself into a state where you act like an oaf, though you're an intelligent, well-read man. You're actually challenging executives to see you as an oaf when you're drunk or stoned so that the next time they think of you for a project, they say to themselves, 'Who needs *that* shmuck?' When you do work, you fool yourself into thinking you're functioning and productive. You have no consciousness of reality." I intellectually grasped everything Dr. Carr was saying to me, but I could not yet accept it. I knew he was right, but I was getting physically tired of the struggle, and I drifted away from him. This was one of the last times I saw him.

I went to Hollywood to do my role in Kramer's *It's a Mad, Mad, Mad, Mad World*, and—at the same time—I had to tape four of the new ABC episodes. That was so the show could get a four-week start in the fall, allowing me a month of rehearsals on Broadway for Doc Simon's *Little Me*. It was a disastrous schedule. In both the movie and the TV series I was there, but it was like I wasn't. I thought I'd enjoy spending time with Mickey Rooney, Phil Silvers, Carl Reiner, and the rest. Instead, I walked through my parts—again mostly on instinct—and drifted off to find oblivion.

When I got back to New York, there was a flash of excitement again as I went into the *Little Me* rehearsals. Whenever I was stimulated by an atmosphere of creativity, I slackened off on my addictions. There was plenty of creativity there, with Neil

Simon's words and Cy Coleman's music. Both leading ladies, Virginia Martin and Nancy Andrews, were very good.

Then we opened—to great reviews. It was a good show, and the critics liked me. They all marveled at my ability to shift physically and mentally from one of the seven characters into another, and some of them even recalled the same type of magic we had created in the live-television days. *Life* did a fold-out cover on "the Seven Caesars." But it wasn't too long before my paranoia and lack of self-esteem took over. As I mentioned before, there was a very fine dancer in the show. His name was Sven Svenson. Every night he'd do a solo dance which would bring down the house. Even though I was getting applause throughout the performance, I'd listen to *his* applause and say to myself, "The people aren't coming to see me. They're coming to see Svenson."

It did not help that I was locked into a back-breaking schedule. I'd do eight shows a week in *Little Me*, and every other week I'd have to spend parts of several days taping the ABC "As Caesar Sees It" series. My weight continued to drop. I looked drawn and haggard, even though I still pursued my old habit of eating a lot and then throwing up. My tolerance for quick absorption of food apparently was diminishing. At the same time, my tolerance for alcohol, sedatives, and tranquilizers seemed to be on the rise.

The series was only a pale shadow of what "Your Show of Shows" had been. ABC, then the lowliest and the poorest of the three networks, was just beginning to experiment with our type of comedy. Their main staple had been filmed Westerns from Warner Brothers, and they were ill-equipped physically and financially for sketch humor. We did two skits in every half-hour show—and that was it.

The Helena Rubinstein sponsorship lasted only nineteen weeks. Then the Consolidated Cigar Company took over and the format of the show was changed. Carl, Howard, and Imogene were gone—replaced by Gisele MacKenzie and Joey Foreman. I barely remember anything about this series, except that Gisele was a lovely and talented lady. The critics said she was one of the best of my television "wives." Too bad I didn't have time to appreciate that. What with doing the Broadway show and the series, I didn't have time to blow my nose.

One other thing stands out in my mind about that ABC series. Our head writer was Goodman Ace, who had been one of my radio heroes when I was a kid growing up in Yonkers. Goody had been one of the great wits of the 1930s—both as a writer and a performer—in his radio show, "Easy Aces." As I watched him working on *our* show, I could see him gradually wilt under the pressure. I felt as if I were holding up a mirror to myself. As we rehearsed, Goody would turn his back to us and just follow the words in the script. Coming from radio, he thought the words were the most important; he did not even see the physical manipulations I did that went beyond the words.

One night, in *Little Me,* the pressure finally did catch up with me. Someone gave me a new, strong tranquilizer. "This will *really* give you a zoom," he said. It gave me more than a zoom. I collapsed on the stage and had to be rushed, unconscious, to Roosevelt Hospital.

But I was gone only one night. I came back and I finished out the run of the show on Broadway. I also finished out the run of the TV series on ABC.

Then Florence—ever trying to come up with something to

help me—dragged me off for three weeks of rest and relaxation in an exotic new atmosphere: Greece. I drank in both the brilliant sunshine and the ouzo.

When I got back, Doc Simon sent me off for another full year on the road in *Little Me*.

Like my son the doctor says, I must have had the constitution and the genes of an ox.

# 20

# Working on Instinct, like a Boxer in the Ring

*Little Me* was "The Last Hurrah" of my Glory Days. Strange that it should have come when my Dark Period already had begun. In 1981 Neil Simon redid the play on Broadway, but with several actors, including James Coco, in the multiple parts I had played. It didn't work. In panning the show, nearly all critics referred back to the original production, in which I had done all the male roles by myself.

My capabilities then, and for several years after that, were residual. I was like a veteran boxer getting in the ring, bobbing and weaving, using all the old footwork, working on instinct,

183

winning a fair number of bouts—but no longer displaying the innovative techniques that had once characterized his skills.

I could not be—or *did* not want to be—part of the creative process that had once so excited and inspired me. People gave me scripts and I did them. I got paid, and that was all that mattered.

I more or less went into seclusion at my home in King's Point. Friends like Larry Gelbart, Mel Brooks, Carl Reiner, dropped away. I can't blame them. I guess I wasn't easy to take in my constant state of semistupor and/or belligerence. This didn't upset me too much. When understanding came many years later, I realized that helping to force the defection of my friends was part of the self-punishment process Dr. Carr had explained to me, but which I was not yet ready to accept. It was in the same category as when Dr. Carr had said to me, "You get drunk or stoned in order to act like an oaf, which leads to producers not giving you work." Before I left him, Dr. Carr explained this phenomenon even further: "When you get turned down for work, you give yourself permission to revert even more to the bottle, which contains one mind-altering chemical or the other. The bottle, thus, is your best and only friend."

Like all alcoholics, I made the mistake of thinking I could help myself by switching from whiskey to wine and beer. It was a studied illusion, mostly to appease Florence into thinking I was making some progress. She was too smart to buy it. Actually, I was consuming as much alcohol as before, only with larger quantities of liquid. Also, I did not slack off on the Equanil, the Seconal, or the other pills. Florence herself had to go to a psychiatrist just to learn how to keep living with me. She didn't want to leave me. She wanted to be there when I needed her. She *had* to be there for the children, who

The children are growing up. Rick *(left)* and Shelly *(right)*.

o work off his aggressions, Sid shoots halvah cans t the Avon Lodge in the Catskills.

Sid's funniest on-camera improvisation in "Your Show of Shows." As he makes up for Pagliacci, his pencil slips and he plays tic-tac-toe on his cheek.

Another opera satire with Imogene.

This "Your Show of Shows" dancer vaulting over Sid
is Mel Brooks's first wife, Florence.

"Your Show of Shows" evolves into
"Caesar's Hour," and Gina Lollobrigida is Sid's
first guest star.

Now it's the team of Nanette Fabray and Sid Caesar, and the
"domestic sketches" are about the Victors
instead of the Hickenloopers

Howard Morris *(left)* and Carl Reiner *(right)* blend in perfectly with Nanette and Sid.

Sid as a gangster in one of his hundreds of impersonations on "Caesar's Hour."

Carl, Sid, and Howard were impeccable in their physical humor.

After the shows, at Danny's Hideaway, Sid (here with proprietor, Danny) usually lost control to booze.

Imogene and Sid at a circus benefit with Marlene Dietrich (*right*).

Taking off for England to do a TV series for the BBC. Florence is holding new baby, Karen. Son Rick is at right. Daughter Shelly is on stairs below Imogene Coca.

Sid (in wheelchair, *center*) stars in Neil Simon's Broadway hit musical *Little Me*, playing seven roles, 1962.

As his Dark Period begins in the mid-1960s, this is how his agents merchandised him for films like *The Busy Body* with Robert Ryan and Anne Baxter.

Sid as Fred Poitrine in *Little Me*.

"I got thin and haggard as my health and my mind deteriorated. I took up painting and sometimes I went back to playing the saxophone by myself."

"In 1975 I went to Australia to do a movie called *Barnaby and Me*. I don't remember anything about the trip or the picture. I lost a whole continent."

"It all was a big black blob. I worked, and I was there, but I really wasn't there." A photographer caught this mood while Sid rehearsed for a nightclub performance.

It wasn't much better when I played the studio executive in Mel Brooks's *Silent Movie* in 1976...

or with John Travolta in *Grease*, 1977...

r at a Dean Martin "roast" in the same year."

The signs of deterioration begin to appear dramatically at the opening of the film *Ten from Your Show of Shows*, which Sid put together with Max Liebman.

Making an appearance on Jerry Lewis's Muscular Dystrophy Telethon in 1978, Sid was barely recognizable in the depths of his Dark Period.

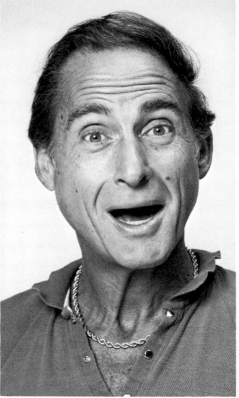

This is how Sid looks today, now fully recovered in body and mind.

(Photo by Karen Caesar)

A recent family reunion. Sid with son-in-law Paul Glad *(left)*, daughter Michele Glad *(center)*, and Florence *(right)*.

Sid at home with his dog, Conus, and bust of George Bernard Shaw.

needed her more than ever. The psychiatrist helped her to survive. So thank God, she was still there when the nightmare finally ended and I needed her support more than ever.

In terms of work, the next several years remain a blur to me. One thing that made me different from many alcoholics and pillheads, I suppose, is that I did manage to pull myself together to go to work from time to time. It was the old work ethic I inherited from my father: no matter how sick a man is, he has to provide for his family. It superseded even my self-punishment obsession.

I went on the road in summer stock. I accepted guest-star shots in other people's TV shows. Again, I was handed scripts and I did them, no matter how inane they were. I didn't care. I even did two movies for William Castle, who then was the master of film schlock. One of them was *The Busy Body* in 1966. I starred in it with Robert Ryan and Anne Baxter. I was barely aware of their existence. As an indication of how I managed to hide my problems from the public, one critic, Steven H. Scheuer, wrote, "Once again, Caesar's superb talents have been wasted by Hollywood." Neither he nor most other people knew that my talents were on hiatus.

In that year, 1966, Florence said to me, "We should move to Los Angeles. That's where most of the work is for you. Besides, the change in environment might help you."

I had been thinking about such a move myself, but I was afraid it would devastate Florence, who had such deep roots in the East. As usual, I had underestimated her strength.

She said, "My parents are here, my sister is here, all my friends are here, the three children are in school here. But I think we should go. There's no question in my mind about it. You should be in the mainstream."

So we went. We sold the big King's Point house, and after

renting for a while in Los Angeles, we bought a much smaller house in Beverly Hills.

There *was* more work for me in Hollywood. I took nearly every one-shot job that came along. Even junk, like the television series "The Munsters." It didn't bother me when people would say, "What's the great Sid Caesar doing in *that* piece of shit?" All that mattered was that I could get it over with quickly and go home to my friend, the bottle. And at least the money kept coming in.

At one point, I figured that with my creativity gone, there was no sense in even continuing as a performer. I went into a business with another man, to promote and advertise show business productions. I was even worse at business than I was at managing my life. My partner wasn't very good at it either. The business went down the drain. So it was back to work again, before the cameras or on the stage.

Because of my remaining name-value, I could always go on the road, for five or six weeks at a time, doing an old Broadway stage play in so-called "dinner theaters." There are a couple of dozen of these dinner theaters around the United States. They bring in a star, surround him with a cast made up of local talent or cheap imported talent from New York or Florida, and then offer a dinner, drinks, and a play for fifteen to twenty dollars a head. I am not denigrating them. They have performed a valuable function in keeping theater interest alive in out-of-the-way places, and as a training ground for young actors and actresses, many of whom, like Polly Holliday, have gone on to Hollywood and Broadway.

In 1972 I latched on to another Neil Simon play, *Last of the Red Hot Lovers*, about a married man with the seven-year itch who unsuccessfully tries to satisfy his extramarital lust with a succession of three young women. It's a funny play, and it was easy for me to learn. Basically, there are only four characters, which made it a natural for the economy-minded dinner-theater circuit. I got a lot of bookings for *Last of the Red Hot Lovers.* I'd show up in a city like Jacksonville, Florida, spend two or three days rehearsing with the director and the cast, and then we'd do our performances (at the Alhambra Theater Restaurant, in this instance) six nights a week, Sunday matinee, no shows on Monday.

So I was on the road a good deal of the time. When Florence could go with me, I more or less was in control. I made a conscious effort, for her sake, to slow down with the booze and the pills. When she couldn't go—if Maranee was away, for example, and not at home to take care of Karen, now a teenager—often there was trouble. I developed an unfortunate habit on airplanes, which always made me uneasy anyway. When I got on board, I'd swallow about six tranquilizers and sleeping pills and wash them down with the booze provided so willingly by the stewardesses. My objective was to sleep through the trip and make it nonpainful.

The problem was that every once in a while, the plane landed and the stewardesses couldn't wake me up. They always thought that maybe I'd had a heart attack or a stroke, and they'd rush me by ambulance to the nearest hospital. There would be calls to my agent or manager, who would call Florence. Poor Florence would then have to get on a plane, sometimes in the middle of the night, to fly to whatever city it was where I was hospitalized. By the time she arrived, I always was all right. I had slept it off, and the doctors were well aware of the nature of my indisposition. Once, this even happened on my way home. From Los Angeles International Airport, the paramedics sped me over to Daniel Freeman Hospital. When the inevitable phone call fetched Florence, she had Karen with her. It was one of the most traumatic experiences of our youngest child's life, and my realization of that actually sobered me completely for a while.

The most extreme of my airplane blackout incidents was the time I was on my way to do the movie *Barnaby and Me* for Norman Panama in Australia, and they couldn't wake me up on that interim stop in New Zealand. By the time Florence arrived in Auckland, I had already recovered and gone on to Sydney. Panama was nervous about my condition, so when Florence arrived in Australia, he prevailed on her to stay on with me. She did, and she got me to work every day, in reasonably usable condition. But as I said, that entire trip remains a total blank in my mind—my Lost Continent. To this day, when I see *Barnaby and Me* in its occasional appearances on cable television, I wonder who *that* Sid Caesar is. *I* certainly wasn't there. None of the backgrounds, none of the sweeping vistas of the beautiful city of Sydney is familiar to me. I find myself criticizing *that* Sid Caesar's performance. If *I* had been there, I would have done such-and-such a scene differently; I would have been a little more subtle with such-and-such a facial expression. I don't know what Florence is talking about when she describes the wonderful things she saw and did when we were in Australia.

*Barnaby and Me* was only one of several movies I did in the 1970s. I remember more about them—but not too much more. There was a film called *Fire Sale,* with Alan Arkin and Rob Reiner, Carl's son. It could have been a good picture if I had known what I was doing. I played a one-legged war veteran riding around in a wheelchair. One day the wheelchair became a runaway and I broke several small bones in my foot trying to stop it before I crashed into a wall.

So when Mel Brooks asked me to play the bewildered studio

executive in his fine film *Silent Movie,* I had to do the entire role sitting down, because of my broken foot. Acting bewildered wasn't too difficult for me. As Mel says, "That was Sid's natural state in those days. I knew what he was going through and I wanted to use him in all my pictures. He would have been marvelous as the Nazi in *The Producers.* The part was typical of what he used to do so brilliantly on 'Your Show of Shows,' and I thought it would help jar him back to himself. But the studio wouldn't let me hire him."

A lot of people tried to help. When I did *Airport 1975,* at Universal with Charlton Heston, Karen Black, and George Kennedy, I had a small part that could have been built up into a meaty one. I remember Jennings Lang, the producer, and Jack Smight, the director, coming over to me on the sound stage and saying, "For God's sake, Sid, use your good brain. Add some *shtick* of your own to this part. Build it up. Create." I couldn't create.

My most painful work experiences of a painful decade came in two of those occasional bright patches in the fog when I *could* create. In 1967 we reassembled all the available elements—writers and performers—of "Your Show of Shows," and we did a TV special starring Imogene, Carl, Howard, and me. In fact, it was called "The Sid Caesar, Imogene Coca, Carl Reiner, Howard Morris Special." It was on CBS and it was a good show. So good, in fact, that nine of us got Emmys for it—Mel Brooks and Mel Tolkin among the writers. We were named "Outstanding Variety Special" of the year, beating out Bob Hope's Christmas Show and Dick Van Dyke.

But CBS never reran our show, not even once.

Then, in 1972, Max Liebman came to me with the idea of assembling a movie called *Ten from Your Show of Shows.* We drove ourselves to put together an hour and a half of some of our best material. It went out into the theaters and got great reviews from the critics. It has become a recurring cult film, which, even today, keeps popping up on television. But when it was first released, our distributor was not experienced in handling mass-market films. The picture never reached an overall national audience.

I thought these echoes of past glory would turn everything around for me.

They didn't.

# 21
# Fight or Flight

My state of mind being what it was during that period, my recollection is not too clear about how terrible I was in my relations with Florence and the children. My family, however, remembers well.

*Florence Caesar*

*Sid could be very terrible at times. Once we were driving along the Santa Monica Freeway in Los Angeles and I said, "Please slow down. You're going too fast." Just an innocent remark like that would throw him into a frenzy. He said, "Fast? I'll show you fast." He then opened up the car until we were going eighty miles an hour, weaving in and out of traffic. He nearly got us killed. And he's an excellent driver when he's sober.*

*He seemed to take out all his frustrations on me. I would become the scapegoat if another motorist cut in front of him, or if an electrician came to the house and did a lousy job of fixing the clothes dryer. He'd yell and scream at me. He'd also yell and scream if I wanted to watch a talk show on TV and he wanted to see a Western.*

*Everything was my fault. Once he got annoyed watching another successful comedian perform, but he held his anger in check until later, when we were playing a word game with some friends. He came up with a name no one recognized. I said, "Oh, it's probably some obscure World War I general." He picked up a heavy club chair and hurled it against the wall. I became the object of his fury about the other comedian, who was more articulate in communicating with live audiences than he was.*

*With the children, he was devastatingly sarcastic. Karen was afraid of him and stayed out of his way. It actually was easier for all of us when he reached the stage when most of the time he'd pass out and be asleep in his chair. But even that was not a sure sign of peace. One night Shelly came home with a young man she was dating. Sid was snoring away in front of the TV set. The rest of us were having a lively discussion about something or another, when suddenly Sid woke up. He said to the young man, "Don't you dare shake your finger at my wife." He then picked him up and shook him. The kid was scared to death and Shelly was crying. It broke up their relationship.*

*Time and time again my friends asked me why I didn't leave Sid. I thought of doing so many times. My own psychiatrist had conditioned me to learn how to live with him for my own self-preservation. It was like they teach you in Al-Anon today.*

*But I couldn't leave Sid, for many reasons. First was the ethic in which I had been brought up. You married a man, and he provided for you, and your job was to take care of him and the children. Like most comedians, Sid was another child. He needed me more than my others did. When he was at his worst, I seemed to be the only one who could straighten him out.*

*Those terrible times, for instance, when I'd be called in the middle of the night to fly somewhere because he was unconscious in a hospital after a plane trip, or because he was falling asleep during the rehearsals of a show on the road. He always was so helpless when I got there. Just my showing up seemed to make him aware that it was an emergency and he'd better pull himself together. He always did. And that was part of my job.*

*Another thing that kept me from leaving was my incurable optimism. As bad as he was—half-stoned most of the time, losing all interest in clothes and walking around like a slob, alienating what friends we had left, constantly criticizing me and the children—I couldn't stop having faith that one day he'd recover from this dreadful disease. I believed in the powers of science and the resiliency of the human mind.*

*I kept bolstering myself with memories of how Sid used to be. I kept myself going by thinking back to things like a song he wrote for me on my twenty-first birthday, when he was in the Coast Guard and had no money, and the song was the only birthday present he could give to me.*

> *I wrote you a song for your*
> *birthday*
> *I wrote it 'cause I want you*
> *to know*

Where Have I Been?

> *That I couldn't buy anything*
> > *real*
> *To show you, darling, just*
> > *how I feel*
> *So I wrote you a song for your*
> > *birthday*
> *I wrote it 'cause I want you*
> > *to know*
> *That I still remember*
> *The third of September*
> *Means happy birthday, dear*
> > *Florence, to you.*

*I couldn't let myself stop believing that that Sid, the Sid who wrote that sweet simple little song, would some day come back.*

*Although he was making it more and more difficult for me to cling to that belief.*

*Perhaps I should have been tougher. Maybe I should have left him. But I kept reading that you should never threaten unless you really mean to do it. I could never reach that decision. I was afraid he would die. And also, Sid would beguile me with his flashes of normality.*

*So my role continued to be that of the rescuer.*


## Rick Caesar

*I'm a physician. In my emergency room practice in Oregon, I've seen twenty-six-year-olds who could not survive even a fraction of the multisubstance abuse to which my father subjected himself. There's a remarkable genetic spectrum for staying alive with his type of addiction. Fortunately, his barrier was very high.*

*When I was a child, his addiction forced me into premature maturity. He was schizoid, in the sense that he was a totally different personality when he was drunk than when he was sober. It was in the interest of any kind of peace in the house that he not be drunk. Being a nonverbal person, he had no backup of expressing what was bothering him. He was like a wounded animal in many ways—or like a child. I had a child for a father.*

*He'd have his temper tantrums, he'd express his insatiable ego, and then, when my mother had given up and had gone to bed, he'd bribe me to stay up with him. The bribe was that he wouldn't drink just so long as I would stay up with him. Then he'd babble on to me in his slurred speech, while I'd yawn and listen to all his anger. He'd tell me, "I can say things to you that I only can say to my psychiatrist."*

*I was all of ten years old then, and I did childish things like hiding his liquor bottles in my room or pouring out half the granules in his drug capsules so he'd be swallowing less barbiturate. It was a pathetically naive way of treating the symptom, not the cause.*

*I grew up to be six feet eleven and became the center on the Beverly Hills High School basketball team. My father was proud of me, but at the same time he was jealous. I was competing with him for public attention. I did not play basketball anymore when I went on to college at Yale. Yet when I saw him, he continued to be abusive and sarcastic to me, as he was with my sisters. He was all right when he was sober or sedated. But when he was drinking, he pouted and sulked; he got loud, obnoxious, and vulgar. The tendency toward violence always was there, and he had surrounded himself with guns—*

*very dangerous stuff. To his credit, however—considering the epidemic of wife and child abuse in this country—he never did any physical harm to us children or to Mother.*

*I have opposite role models to the norm. My mother was the tower of strength in the family—in a low-key, understated way. She epitomized tolerance, power, consistency, cheerfulness, and altruism. To this day I probably unrealistically idealize women, and I'm impatient and critical with most American men. Too many of them are like my father. With their hunting, dune-buggy races, and so on, it's all sort of a wild celebration of the ego. But it's really a compensation for latent insecurity.*

*My own choice of profession is related to what I saw my father's profession do to him. The instability, the fickleness of it all. He'd stumble into my room at night, reeking of what he'd been drinking, and he'd mumble, "Be a fireman. Be a baseball player." I had been an English major at Yale and I had done some writing, which I really liked, but I decided on what would be the greatest possible divergence from my father's career: I went on to study medicine at the University of California, Davis.*

*It was now the late 1970s. Things seemed to be getting worse whenever I got home. My father would scream and yell and make a big scene. Or he'd fall on his face and vomit all over himself. Or in a fit of rage, he'd pick up a television set and hurl it into the swimming pool.*

*The next day he'd be repentant and we'd have discussions. He'd say, "Maybe there's some treatment somewhere." I'd tell him that what he needed was a modern detoxification unit and chemical dependency treatment center in a good hospital. He always backed away from the idea. Maybe it was a throwback to his childhood, when the immigrant ethic was to keep such problems quiet and within the family. Maybe it was the old fears, instilled in him by the studios of his Big Star days, that no such hospital was secure in terms of leaks to the press (not true, of course). Maybe it was his experiences with private psychiatrists, which in his mind (but not in mine) had been almost wholly unproductive.*

*In any event, after each such episode of bad behavior, he'd be OK for a few days.*

## Michele Caesar

*I'm sure my father loved me and I loved him, but we never had much of a relationship. When I was a child, I was puzzled by his celebrity. Occasionally on a Sunday he'd take me to an amusement park called Kiddie City on Long Island. I couldn't understand it when people stole French-fried potatoes off his plate as souvenirs.*

*As I became a teenager, I became aware of how irrational he could be at times. Mother was taking things one day at a time. She acted as a buffer between me and Dad. But one night, when she wasn't home, I had to ask his permission to go to a party at a next-door neighbor's house. The party was supposed to start at nine o'clock. He said, "OK, but you have to be home at ten." I didn't get back until midnight. He went berserk. He ripped off a couple of doorknobs and that was one of the times he tore a sink right out of a wall.*

*I graduated from North High School in Great Neck and went to Southampton College. Dad never was involved with me unless I wanted to see my boyfriend, when he'd automatically say no. I'd bring the boy home and Dad would say crazy things to him, like, "OK, if you love her, go downstairs and shoot off your foot." I didn't even like the boy very much, but there was so much pressure on me that I soon married another young man, Henry. I was only nineteen. I was much too young. My new husband was a leather-goods salesman and he wanted me to be on the road with him for most of the year. When the marriage inevitably broke up, I rejoined my parents in Beverly Hills.*

*I went to Santa Monica College and then to UCLA. I was in the music department, and after I got my B.A. degree, I went on to graduate school to get a teaching certificate so I could work with disadvantaged children and make them realize the ties between their own rock-and-roll and good classical music. I knew what a fine musician my father had been, but he never would discuss music with me. Maybe it was because he had drifted away from music as a young man and now regretted it. He wanted me to be an artist because he was studying painting and his teacher had told him one of the woodcuts I had done in Long Island was very good. I eventually did become an artist, by my own choice. The medium I work in is stained glass. I've done quite well and my pieces sell. But Dad was furious about my choice of medium from the very beginning. He'd say, "What kind of art form is that?" Stained-glass sculptures did not fit into one of his pigeonholes of acceptability.*

*I only lived at home for eight months. It was too depressing. I got my own apartment and eventually I married again, to Paul Glad, an attorney. Mother and Dad gave us the biggest, most expensive wedding at the Bel Air Hotel. Dad never deprived us of material things. It was his way of making amends, I guess.*

*I continued to visit my parents after my marriage and witnessed Dad's continuing deterioration. He felt let down by so many people that he was taking it out on himself in a very destructive way. He'd say to us kids, "Go get me four and four." That meant four barbiturates and four tranquilizers. Then he'd pass out. Eventually he was up to "eight and eight." When he was conscious and also drinking, he'd get very aggressive about the silliest things. If he was watching a football game and the cable went out, he'd curse and scream that the cable company was doing it to him personally. He'd become enraged if we watched a young comedian like John Belushi on TV and we dared to laugh. If he only knew that Belushi also was destroying himself in a very similar way.*

*For all he had done to us kids, by omission and commission, my heart went out to my father as I watched him gradually sink into becoming a hermit. But we couldn't communicate.*

## Karen Caesar

*I'm the youngest, born in 1956, and I wasn't too aware of what was going on when I was a child. In those years, my perception was of my father falling asleep at the dinner table or throwing up all over himself. I never really understood or wanted to understand what was happening. I remember hushed conversations between my mother and my brother: "Did he take four and six?" "No, he only took two and two." Until I was well into my teens, I didn't know what that meant. It was disturbing to me. I was kept out of it: "Karen, she's too young to understand."*

*When I was in junior high school, Dad went to bed once and didn't wake up for three days. I was terrified. Everyone else had parents who were up. I wrote a letter to my brother Rick at Yale asking, "What's going on here?" He wrote me a very soothing letter, explaining Dad's problems in detail for the first time. Then Mother decided she'd better fill me in, too, about Dad's drinking and his pills. I almost wished I didn't have to be told.*

*I consider that I was raised with two parents—Mom and Maranee, our housekeeper. I felt deprived, though Mom tried to fill the void. She hates meetings, but she came to every function at school. Nevertheless, I wished I had a father who was interested. I was a pretty smart kid, with an A average; I was on the school paper, and I was selected for a student exchange program in Switzerland for three months. I'd say to Mom, "Why tell Dad? He'll only forget." I loved him, but it always was like not seeing a friend for three years, and there was always so much to catch up on, and no time. Sometimes I'd call the house and he'd answer the phone and say, "Karen? Karen who?"*

*As for his aggressiveness when he was inebriated, Mom and Rick took the brunt of it. Shelly was sort of out of it, floating around with friends and then getting married again. She understandably didn't want to be at home when Dad would pick up a chair and threaten to throw it at Mom, which he never did. It was for show. With me, I'd ask to be excused from the table, and he'd slam his fist on the table and roar, "No!" Or he'd suddenly demand my presence for no reason at all. It was frightening.*

*When it comes to choosing between fight and flight, I always fall back on flight. Even in intellectual arguments with my brother, whom I adore, I usually opt for flight. It was the same when I heard my father start his screaming and yelling. I'd hide in my room, usually in the bathroom or closet. We had a wonderful sweet dog named Cindy—part German shepherd, part collie—who'd also run into my room when the trouble began. She'd cower with me in my closet, and we'd both cry in the dark.*

200

*I remember some interesting things. For example, Rick would never watch Dad when he was on television. It hurt my dad. I understand Rick's attitude and yet I don't. I think it would kill Rick to see the audience not react to Dad the way they should. When Dad was on with Johnny Carson or Merv Griffin, Mom would sit two feet from the screen and be nervous. Rick would stay out of the room. I would walk in and out of the room—hoping for laughs.*

*I missed a lot of the darkest of Dad's dark period because I was away at college from 1975 to 1979. I went to Stanford, where my grades continued to be very good. I was a journalism major, on the staff of the* Stanford Daily, *one of the best college newspapers in the country, for four years. Once again, I was chosen for a foreign study program and went to Austria and England. I graduated high in my class, but Dad didn't come to my commencement.*

*I guess it's a miracle that all three of us kids turned out as well as we did. None of us is a boozer or a doper. My brother is a respected physician; my sister is a respected artist with her stained-glass sculptures. I'm in politics. I'm press aide to a Los Angeles county supervisor, Ed Edelman.*

*We all have our scars. But as Rick says, "We must have the same tough genes that kept Dad alive and eventually enabled him to pull out of it."*

# 22
# Bottoming Out

In 1977 I guess I was not too conscious of my family's perceptions of me. I was not too conscious of *anything*, except that I now was in the darkest of my dark period. I kept having that recurrent infant image of no hands on the carriage. Except that my brother Dave's rope was gone, too, and the baby carriage, instead of being stopped at the end of the rope, was rolling wildly all the way down to the bottom of the hill. The bottom. In my baby mind, what could it be but an abyss.

Only one fairly positive thought came filtering through. As an amateur student of economic theory, I knew that every recession—even a depression—bottoms out. Only then does recovery begin.

I kept trying to work. Imogene Coca and I got booked into

the Sahara Hotel in Las Vegas. We put together some of our old routines from "Your Show of Shows," but once again I wasn't all there. Besides, the hotel coupled our act with Eddy Arnold. He's a great entertainer. However, combining him with us on the same bill must represent one of the most inept programming decisions of all time. His country-western music audience had nothing in common with us. They didn't come to hear our brand of subtle satire, and we could not do a Blues Brothers act for them.

It was not what you would call a rousing success. It got better later when they moved us into a dinner show-midnight show rotation with Jerry Lewis and Buddy Hackett. *Those* audiences did like us and stimulated me. But then Imogene had to leave to do a show in New York and our reteaming was over. Emotionally, I was now primed to hit bottom.

Bottom consisted of my going home and never leaving the house for all of January, February, March, and April of 1978— not even for a haircut. I hardly ever got out of bed. I had stocked up on pills—having coaxed prescriptions out of the many doctors I went to, all of whom were worried about my enlarged liver and still were mistakenly gambling on anything that might substitute for the alcohol. I had been conning them for years, and they didn't know it. More likely, the easiest way for a doctor to get rid of a difficult patient is to just give him a prescription for anything he wants. That's one of the problems of modern medicine, especially in an affluent, high-rent-for-doctors area like Beverly Hills.

Needless to say, I had plenty of alcohol to go with my pills. Florence and Maranee got rid of the liquor bottles (the pill bottles, which were easier to hide, had been stashed by me all over the house), but I could get plenty of beer. Florence and Maranee couldn't watch me every minute, and all I had to do was telephone our local market and they'd send over a case of six-packs.

When I was conscious during this period, I thought constantly of suicide. I knew I was committing slow suicide anyway, but I kept considering cleaner, faster methods. There is a winding road called Mulholland Drive that wanders along the top of the Santa Monica Mountains that bisect the city of Los Angeles. There are steep cliffs on both sides of Mulholland, some of them dropping off for hundreds of feet into deep ravines. I didn't live too far from Mulholland Drive. How easy it would be to get into my car and just let it roll gently over one of those cliffs. But I wasn't too far gone to let one thing stop me. Suppose I couldn't quite make it look like an accident? I had a vague recollection of suicide clauses in insurance policies, and what if the insurance companies wouldn't pay off to Florence and the children?

Florence wisely left me alone. Maranee saw to it that I got enough food to sustain me. I think they realized I was going through a crisis that only I could resolve, and that doctors could not help me at this point. Even so, I kept thinking back to my therapy sessions with Dr. Carr, the only psychiatrist to whom I'd ever been able to relate. I remember saying to Dr. Carr, "You're such a kind and understanding man that I want to stop the booze and the pills for *you*."

He'd said, "You can't stop for me. You can't stop for your father, whom I represent in your mind. You can't stop for Florence or your children or for anyone else in the world. You won't stop until you realize you have to do it for *you*. Yes, as selfish as it sounds, *only* for you. After that, your concerns for others will rightfully fall into place."

I'd said, "And when will that be, doctor?"

"When you finally realize that you don't *deserve* all the

guilts, the self-punishment, the destructiveness you're inflicting on yourself. That you *do* have talents few other people possess. That you *are* worthy of the good things that have happened to you. That it wasn't just some kind of miracle."

I still didn't understand it, but the thoughts kept percolating around in my head.

Along with a lot of other not-so-positive thoughts.

I was consumed with irrational envy. So many of the people who had worked for me had gone on to one major success after another. Doc Simon's plays and movies kept coming out at a rate of about two a year; Mel Brooks's films were enormous hits; Carl Reiner was a major producer and director; Larry Gelbart, after developing "M-A-S-H," one of the best series in the history of TV, was doing *Sly Fox* on Broadway and the George Burns-John Denver movie, *Oh, God!* ; Lucille Kallen was turning out novels; Mel Tolkin had been a key writer on "All in the Family," another television milestone.

And there were all the new young comedians—Chevy Chase, Steve Martin, Robin Williams, John Belushi, Dan Aykroyd, Gilda Radner. I found much of their humor unfunny, unfinished—playing for one line or one physical shock, instead of telling a story. I irrationally hated them. I liked only Richard Pryor, George Carlin, and Robert Klein (who reminded me of me). I liked an occasional coherent skit of the SCTV group. "Saturday Night Live" turned me off completely. In movies I couldn't see the humor in water spouting out of countless hydrants hit by countless cars.

My daughter Shelly once made an interesting point when, as usual, I was just half-listening to her. Speaking as a musicologist, she said, "You are like Beethoven, who took all the classical forms of music and stretched them to a point no one had ever reached before. After Beethoven came Ravel and Sibelius, who created new forms of music. In comedy, you are a classicist. The new comics have moved in other directions. But Beethoven and Ravel *both* are still played in the concert halls. Why don't you think of the two forms of comedy in the same way?"

In my state of confused misery, I couldn't think rationally about anything. I wasn't watching television. I wasn't reading the newspapers. I really wanted to die, but my own physical strength betrayed me. I couldn't even do that right.

From time to time, I thought about the kids. I didn't even know where they were or what they were doing. I figured that if something were wrong, Florence would take care of it.

Florence brought me books on subjects she knew interested me—history, physics, economics. I'd read, take a few of my pills, and pass out. But I'd leave a book open on the bed to make her think I was still reading, and that maybe tomorrow I'd get up.

My big accomplishment of the day was forcing myself to get into the bathroom and take a shower. When I shaved, I counted the razor strokes; I measured the exact amount of hot water I used.

I heard the normal sounds of the house—vacuuming, dogs barking, telephones ringing, Maranee's pots clattering in the kitchen— and I thought, "Those are such nice normal sounds. I wish I could get up and be part of those house-sounds." I couldn't.

It wasn't until early in May that I came out of my cocoon. My agent called and asked if I wanted to do *Last of the Red Hot Lovers* in Canada.

Florence said, "Go. But I'm not going with you this time.

You've got a lot more thinking to do, and you have to work it out alone."

So I went to Regina, Saskatchewan. I kept myself together during rehearsals. Then, the night before the play was to open, I felt I had to fly back to Los Angeles for an affair honoring Max Liebman and "Your Show of Shows." I took my pills on the flight down and also on the flight back to Regina.

That's when I found—on opening night—that, for the first time in my life, I could be "conscious" on a stage and not remember my lines or cues or what I was supposed to be doing.

That's when I went back to my crummy little dressing room off the kitchen of the Hotel Regina and came to that split second in which I had to decide whether I wanted to live or die.

That's when I opted for life and told Henry, my ex-busboy dresser, to send for the hotel physician, Dr. LeBlond.

That's when I said to Dr. LeBlond, "This is it. Please help me"—and he rushed me to Regina General Hospital.

And that's when my own personal twenty-year Great Depression bottomed out—and the recovery process finally could begin.

# 23

# "OK, I Give Up. I've Had Enough Punishment"

My first few days in Regina General were a nightmare. In addiction-alcoholism cases, Canadian methods are much different from ours. They believe in total cold turkey. The first thing ordered by Dr. LeBlond and his colleague, Dr. Sinclair, was that I be taken off *all* pills. They even took my vitamins away from me. No gradual withdrawal here. If I went into convulsions (barbiturate withdrawal can be even more deadly than heroin withdrawal), they would deal with that with the proper medications—if and when it happened.

It didn't happen. But I was climbing the walls for nearly

a week. It was absolute torture. I kept watching the clock, day and night: "It's 2:05, it's 2:08, it's 2:09 and an eighth, it's 2:09 and a quarter. . . ." The nurses kept watching *me* to make sure I didn't convulse.

I was weak and dizzy. I said to Dr. LeBlond, "Can't I at least have my vitamins to help get me through this?"

He said, "No. We want you to get out of the habit of taking all pills—of any kind."

I said, "OK, but how about sleep? I just can't sleep."

He said, "So you're not going to sleep for a while. It won't kill you."

He wasn't telling me anything I didn't know. Dr. Carr had said the same things many years before, but at that time I wasn't yet ready to accept them. Now I was. I had had the biggest and best doctors, and they all had told me not to do what I was doing and I'd always find a way to outfox them. Here, a provincial doctor in Canada said, "No more pills no matter how little sleep you get," and I obeyed him. I could have found a way to get around his orders. Prowling the hospital at night, I could have found an unattended nurse's cart in the corridors with a little paper cup of barbiturates prescribed for someone else.

But this time I didn't want to find a way.

I knew the dangers. Dr. LeBlond didn't have to explain them to me. When you drink and take pills you can die. I was aware of that long before the Dorothy Kilgallen and Marilyn Monroe tragedies. In fact, that's why I was doing it. You play with death. You come as close to it as you can.

There was no magic in Dr. LeBlond's method. It's just that the timing was right. Now that I had decided to live, I didn't want to outfox anyone anymore. I didn't have the strength anymore to go on as I had.

Where Have I Been?

As I sat up night after night in that Regina hospital, I was saying to myself, "OK, that's enough. I give up. I've had enough punishment. Let the doctors take over. I'm tired of the pills because they have been dominating my whole life." The main thing on my mind was: "Have I got the pills for tonight? Have I got the pills for tomorrow? Do I have enough pills for the rest of this week? Or maybe I'll take two more pills and get a *deeper* sleep. And if I add some booze, it will be even better."

I didn't want to think about that kind of slavery anymore. Wow! What a big relief. But it didn't come right away. It comes in stages, in dribs and drabs, and you get very discouraged.

At the end of seven days in the hospital, I had slept a total of maybe two hours, but Dr. LeBlond's tests showed that I was detoxified. He was amazed. It usually takes much longer for those in the condition I was in. I was very thin and drawn. I looked sick. I had been in a gradual physical deterioration ever since the traumatic day in 1958 when I was told that "Caesar's Hour" was being canceled and being replaced with a can of tape under Robert Kintner's arm. My weight had dropped from 240 to about 175.

Dr. LeBlond said, "Let's see if you can go back to the hotel and do your show." I was scared to death, but I said, "I'll give it a try." The dinner theater rescheduled the opening of the play, and after a couple of rehearsals, we were ready to go again. Opening night went fine and we settled into the regular run of daily after-dinner performances. Dr. LeBlond dropped by every day to see how I was doing. He was a concerned man. He felt for me. He was the only doctor to do so since Sidney Carr.

I did have some lapses in memory onstage, but the cast

was a good one and they filled in for me when I dropped a line. Or I'd improvise and just blend in with the general sense of the plot. After four weeks, Dr. LeBlond, who knew the play by heart by this time, apparently noticed this and he asked, "Are you sleeping yet?" It was more than a month since I had entered the hospital and I was still unable to more than doze for maybe a half hour at a time. I said, "No, I still can't sleep," and he doled out a single five-milligram Valium tablet, the lowest-dosage tranquilizer there is. That night I got *some* sleep. The next day he gave me another five-milligram Valium, and the following day he got generous and handed me a vial with seven Valiums in it.

He said, "One a day. If you take more than that, you'll run out before the week is over, and even if you hold me up with a gun, I won't give you any more." I took just one a day, and my sleep patterns improved. I thought of doctors in the United States who had given me fifty pills at a time and then told me to come back the following week for another prescription. Each office visit meant more money for them. Dr. LeBlond was not interested in making money that way.

Florence came to Canada, to be with me for a while. She couldn't believe how lucid I was and that I was not drinking at all, and that my "eight and eight" had dwindled down to a precious one. She was still skeptical because I'd had periods of improvement before—or so she had thought. She left to attend Karen's graduation at Stanford, and my brother Dave arrived to take over for her. He, too, was amazed but skeptical.

In the fifth week, Dr. LeBlond said to me, "Your physical condition is deplorable. You need some exercise. Go out and take some long walks. Don't just hang around your room reading." The next morning I saw the first sign of health in myself.

211

I started to go out for a walk, as Dr. LeBlond had suggested, but instead, I looked down at the carpet on the floor of the hotel room and thought for a minute. Then I slowly and awkwardly got myself down on the floor. I stretched out on my back and tried to do some leg-ups and push-ups. I could do only one of each at first, but I kept at it until I had done four or five.

It was my first exercise since I had stopped going to the Gotham Gym in New York when I was twenty-eight years old. I was well into the booze by then and I had just stopped, saying, "The hell with it." It was nothing for me to do fifty or more push-ups before I gave up on the whole idea of keeping in shape.

Now, in Regina, I kept stuggling away on the floor of my hotel room every morning until I could do eight, nine, and finally ten push-ups. Believe me, it was quite an accomplishment for that stage of my life.

Dr. LeBlond was very proud of me for my ten lousy push-ups. When the run of my show was over and he came to say good-bye, we had a nice little talk. I didn't verbalize much with him. I had already gone through that with the psychiatrists. But as we chatted about health in general, my mind focused on many things I already knew. He's a lovely, totally dedicated man and I was fortunate indeed to have known him.

When I got back to Los Angeles, I set about rearranging my whole life. I still had cravings for pills and booze, but I knew I couldn't handle either of them. It was like the great baseball pitcher Don Newcombe once said about his recovery from alcoholism: "I cannot do this anymore. For me, it's poison—like going into the kitchen and drinking a can of lye. Other people can tolerate alcohol, but I can't."

I had known this about myself for a long time, but I still

wasn't over my need for punishing myself. I now had accepted the fact that I am allergic to alcohol and pills, just as others are dangerously allergic to bee-stings and mushrooms. If other people drink or drop Valium in my presence, I'm not a prude. I say, "If you can handle it and control it, fine. *I* can't."

But I also realized I had developed a very addictive personality over the years. My life was one big habit. I brush my teeth with my right hand; I hold the water glass in my left hand. So why not adopt *good* habits if you have an addiction? That's what I did. I substituted a positive addiction for a negative addiction. As dedicated as I was to booze and pills, I dedicated myself to the health of my body and what I put into it in the way of food. Beginning with those few pathetic push-ups on the floor of my hotel room in Regina, I *used* my addiction-prone personality for something good rather than something bad.

I joined a health club in Beverly Hills on November 1, 1978.

I remember the date because it has become very important to me.

# 24

# Relapse

I was on the right track, but I still was a long way out of the woods.

Dr. LeBlond had said, "First repair the body. Then when the body is strong again, it will be easier for you to work on repairing the mind."

I also had read about a case, remarkably similar to mine, which is one of the classic successes of Dr. Joseph A. Pursch of the Long Beach Naval Hospital. Dr. Pursch is considered one of the leading alcoholism-addiction experts in the world, and it was he who helped First Lady Betty Ford recover from booze and pills.

The case he wrote about concerned a successful executive named Ray:

Ray was a man who was endowed with an unusually healthy constitution, which, for many years, enabled him to abuse his body and psyche by alcohol excess and workaholism. Actually his life was tenuously balanced on work and booze.

Ray drank heavily but he always was on the job and had no hangovers. He was admired for his strong constitution. He could really handle his booze. Later, as president of his company, he was known throughout the industry as a bona fide workaholic and a heavy social drinker. Outwardly a great success, he was really leading a very narrow life because work and booze were his only defenses.

Six months after he stopped working, Ray was drinking around the clock and neglecting himself. He was arrested for sleeping in his car. He also had high blood pressure, liver damage, early diabetes, and evidence of alcohol poisoning of his bone marrow. Ray obviously was going to die if he didn't stop drinking.*

Ray came under Dr. Pursch's care at the hospital. He began therapy, and so did his family, who learned how to give him the support he needed. I was so interested in Ray's story that I was disappointed when Dr. Pursch did not go into the details of *why* Ray inflicted so much punishment on himself—as *I* had.

But, at the time, the most significant part of the case to me was Dr. Pursch's conclusion about one of the key factors that contributed to Ray's recovery: "He replaced his alcoholism and workaholism with *sports activities* which he had discontinued over the years, as drinking and working had become the mainstays of his life."

* From Joseph A. Pursch, "Advice on Alcohol," *Los Angeles Times.*

So I *was* on the right track.

I went to the gym every day from 3:00 to 5:00 P.M., and I pushed myself to my physical limits. I lifted weights, I did push-ups and leg-ups, I worked out on every device they had in the gym. My muscle tone began to improve. I gained weight. I began to look like myself again.

I think that when I first arrived at the gym, I was so thin and wan that my fellow exercisers didn't even think I was *that* Sid Caesar. As I began to resemble the old me, I was flattered and pleased that people remembered me and told me how young I looked. I was even more pleased when they would recall certain routines that had been their favorites when they had watched me on "Your Show of Shows," and they asked me to do them for them on the spot.

One guy said, "Hey, Sid, how about that monologue you did about the guy going on a diet?" I was amazed that my mind already had improved to such an extent that I could remember it—at least the beginning part. I did it for him:

Look how chubby I am . . . look at my ears, how fat they are. My eyeballs don't even fit in their sockets anymore. And look at this jacket. It used to be a top coat. . . . Yep, today's the day I'm gonna do it. . . . Today's the day I'm going on a diet. . . . I gotta have will power. . . . I gotta be strong. . . . And you gotta have a lot of strength. . . . So make me a big breakfast 'cause I gotta have a lot of strength to go with this diet.

Diet was on the minds of most of the people in the gym. One tubby fellow in his thirties begged me to do my Professor routine on the subject of you are what you eat. I asked the kid how he possibly could have seen the skit and he said,

"Oh, I don't know. Maybe on some awards show or on public television. That stuff of yours keeps popping up and I love it."

So I racked my brain and came up with what I could remember of Carl Reiner's interview of Professor Kurt von Stuffer, author of *Food Can Be Habit Forming.*

> When a person eats fluffy food, little cakes, pastry, and fancy little things, then that person is also fluffy. But when you eat meats and strong, heavy food, then you also are a strong person. I had a patient once who was so fluffy, so light, that I prescribed a diet of meats and strong foods, and in a couple of months, the patient was six feet tall with muscles and a big, flowing moustache.

Reiner, the interviewer, said, "That's wonderful." I said:

> No, that's terrible. She was a woman and her husband didn't like it.

Actually, all this byplay in the gym was pertinent because I was in the process of completely changing my own diet— although not along the lines suggested by the Professor.

I had given a lot of thought to my deplorable old eating habits and probably associated my past gluttony with the boozing that accompanied it. I remembered with horror the double sirloin steaks, the Stage Delicatessen pastrami sandwiches heaped six inches high with fatty meat, the calorie-loaded Lindy's restaurant cheesecake, the baked potatoes buried under layers of butter, sour cream, and chives. No wonder I had swelled up to 240 pounds—even with all my vomiting.

With the new healthy body I was developing, all such excesses had to go. I didn't trust diet books (I already had plans to satirize them in some future sketch), so I did research in medical journals and devised my *own* diet. It is a regimen I follow to this day.

I eliminated all red meats. The only animal protein I eat is poultry and fish. Also, I limit myself to just two meals a day. I do not eat breakfast until I've done light exercise and my chores around the house and the garden. That means I have no food until about 11:30 A.M.

I begin with a whole grapefruit and a glass of orange juice. Then I have a bowl of oatmeal, sweetened with honey. Next comes a helping of canned fish—tuna, salmon, or kippers— with a slice of whole-wheat bread. Dessert is my own special concoction. It's a mush made of dry cereal, low-fat yogurt, chopped walnuts, raisins, bananas, strawberries, and other fresh or canned fruits. I taught Maranee how to make it and she keeps a bowl of it going in the refrigerator, adding to it constantly the way a French farm-wife keeps soup going on the kitchen stove.

At night, I eat turkey, chicken, with vegetables—followed by my mush for dessert. In restaurants—I prefer Chinese and Japanese—once again it's always poultry or seafood with veg- etables. I wait until I get home to eat my mush for dessert. It's also my late-night snack before I go to bed. When I'm working on the road, the first thing I do is make friends with my hotel's chef (I still speak the restaurant language from my days in my father's luncheonette) and I teach him how to make my mush. He then keeps it on tap for me at all times.

With my diet and my exercise program in full swing, I thought I had it made by the end of November 1978. I hadn't felt so good since I was a teenager. I was looking better every

day. I was keeping myself so busy with my physical rehabilitation that I didn't think much about booze anymore. I no
longer had to take even a single Valium in order to be able
to sleep at night. I was beginning to make the first gropings
in the direction of my next step—the repair of the mind.

I was so confident that I fell into a very common trap. I
made the same mistake that many alcoholics make. There
was a holiday coming up, a big festive gathering, and I was
doing so well. So what could it hurt if I busted loose with
some wine to celebrate? Just one night. What harm could
there be? That's what they *all* say.

So I had a relapse. Not uncommon. But it was a terrible,
terrible experience.

That Thanksgiving started pleasantly enough. Karen had
come home from Stanford, and Rick was down from medical
school at Davis to spend his entire holiday vacation with us.
Shelly was there with her husband, Paul. So were my brothers,
Abe and Dave, and a woman friend of Florence's.

We all chatted away while Maranee put the finishing touches
on one of her superb Thanksgiving dinners. While we talked,
I had a glass of Beaujolais. Then another. I hadn't seen Rick
in some time and I was telling him all about my workouts in
the gym and my new diet. He kept looking uneasily at the
glass in my hand but didn't say anything.

Maranee called us to dinner and we all sat down at the
table. Everything looked beautiful. I filled my glass with
Chablis and toasted Maranee for what a great job she had
done. Then I filled my glass again and toasted everyone else.
We began to eat. Once again, my memory is not too clear
about what happened after that, though it is all *too* clear to
my family.

Where Have I Been?

## Florence Caesar

*I was at the end of the table talking to my friend, when I heard an uproar down where Sid and Rick were sitting. Sid was drinking wine and cursing. I hadn't heard him use bad language like that since before he went to Canada. Rick said, "Don't talk like that or I'm not going to stay around."*

*Sid cursed some more and Rick got up to leave. Sid yelled, "Get back here."*

*Rick said, "I'm going to pack, and get in my van, and I'm going to stay at Shelly's house in Venice."*

*I jumped in to try and calm things down, but it was too late. Sid was hollering, like in the old days. Shelly and Karen were both crying. They kept saying, "Daddy, stop." Maranee was in the middle of the whole thing, really chewing Sid out. Everything was bedlam.*

*It was like an Italian movie.*

## Rick Caesar

*Mother tends to talk in terms like that, but it was a lot more serious than just another Italian movie. My father had taken two steps forward since Canada, and now he had taken one step back. He had reverted to childlike aggression.*

*It was the wine that did it. From a physiological standpoint, he had lost his tolerance to alcohol in the six months since he stopped drinking. That means he was healing. The liver is a remarkable and dynamic organ. After a period of abstinence—sometimes years, sometimes just several weeks—those liver enzymes that metabolize alcohol go back to normal. So you pour in some wine and you get drunk, like everyone else. All the tolerance to alcohol built up over the years of drinking is gone.*

*So my father's jealousies and feelings of insecurity reemerged at that dinner table. The family hadn't seen me in some time, and they were interested in my experiences at medical school, so Dad wasn't getting all the attention. He began telling stories of his own prowess, using locker-room talk. Because of him, I'm particularly sensitive to bravado. He also was making uncalled-for comments to one of his brothers. I let him know that. At the moment, I figured it was just as well if I never interacted with him again.*

*So I announced I was leaving. That infuriated him even more.*

## Karen Caesar

*What a night that was! After all the yelling and screaming, Rick stormed out of the house. I ran after him and ended up chasing him down the street. I finally convinced him to come back, get his clothes, and make a graceful departure.*

*From outside the house, we could still hear Dad carrying on. I was hysterical. I was afraid my father was going to kill my brother. Rick, who is almost as big as Kareem Abdul-Jabbar, said, "No way." But I made him climb the hill next to the house until things calmed down, and we sat in the ivy behind a tree. I heard Dad come out and get in his car. I got hysterical again. I thought he was going to drive up the hill and try to run us over.*

# Where Have I Been?

## Michele Caesar

*The funny things you remember from times like that. What sticks in my mind is that Dad was swearing at the table and Rick said, "Would you mind not talking like that? I'm trying to eat my mashed potatoes."*

*That line—which could have been from an old Italian movie— is what provoked the entire flap. But there had been a lot of tension between Rick and Dad just before that. Rick obviously decided he wasn't going to put up with Dad's self-indulgent behavior anymore. So he made the remark about his mashed potatoes. Dad flew into a rage. Eventually he became incoherent.*

*Rick left. Mom and Maranee tried to pacify Dad. Then he went outside, too. After a while I saw him outside throwing chairs into the pool. I knew from experience that the only way to stop that kind of behavior was to act crazier than he was. So I ran out to the patio and I began throwing chairs into the pool. The strategy is to get him to stop focusing on himself and to worry about someone else.*

*He looked across at me and said, "Why are you doing that?" Suddenly he became very calm. He put his arm around me and tenderly walked me back into the house.*

The next morning Florence and Karen and Maranee weren't talking to me. I finally got someone to tell me where Rick was. He had gone to Shelly's place out at the beach in Venice.

I had a terrible hangover—not like in the old days—and both physically and emotionally, I've never felt more miserable in my life. I couldn't remember too many of the details, but I knew instinctively what I had done. Two steps forward and one step back, that's what Rick had said. What a step back! I couldn't afford another one like that.

I went out on the back patio and lifted weights. I swam about twenty laps in the pool. That's all I could do. Ordinarily, I'd been doing fifty laps just to warm up.

Finally I called Shelly's house. I asked to speak to Rick, but at first he wouldn't come to the phone. After a while, he got on the line and I apologized. I told him how sorry I was. He said, "OK, Dad," but I didn't see him again for a long time. It was more than a year before we were reconciled.

In a way, the estrangement turned out to be a good thing for me. I agonized over it.

And it made me realize more than ever that I had to get on with the second stage of my rehabilitation: the repairing of the mind, as well as the body.

# 25
# Sid and Sidney

The repair of the mind. Some alcoholics and addicts do it through organizations like Alcoholics Anonymous. Some do it through therapy programs at chemical dependency centers in hospitals. A few manage to "white knuckle it" by themselves.

*I* went to Paris.

That's not as frivolous as it sounds. I had a definite purpose in mind. After the Thanksgiving Day fiasco, I knew for sure that alcohol is poison to me physically, but there was more to it than that. What was there in my head that made me act so bizarrely and go so far in my aggression that I estranged my son? Why did I have to keep wondering why my daughters put up with me and, especially, why Florence didn't just walk out.

I knew, from all the therapy I'd had, that the key to my complete recovery was "making friends with myself." But I'd verbalized my problems too many times to too many psychiatrists and doctors. It hadn't worked. I was all talked out. I didn't think that continuing to talk to other people—even in A.A. or in a hospital group—could help me anymore. I knew the answers by heart. The ritual. On me, it didn't work.

No, the understanding had to come from within myself. I had to wait for an opportunity to get away, alone; preferably to some foreign country where I didn't know the language and there would be nobody to talk to but Sid Caesar. Only then, I reasoned, could I get to the roots of my fears, and my rages, and my insecurities—and convince the part of me that always had resisted comprehension to make friends with the rest of me. This proposed technique was purely instinctive on my part. I had my doubts. Maybe I was embarking on a freaky enterprise. But I later learned that I had stumbled on a method, campatible with the theories of the great pioneering psychiatrist Carl Gustav Jung, which had helped other people like me. So once again, without realizing it, I was not alone. The question was: Would it work in my case?

I knew the process would take a long time, so I waited for a foreign movie assignment to come along—one that would force me to be with only myself for weeks and even months. This prospect in itself frightened me, but I knew it had to be done. Then my agent called and said there was a part for me in a Peter Sellers movie, *The Diabolical Plot of Dr. Fu Manchu*, with a five-month shooting schedule in France. He said the picture would not exactly be a work of art, but without a moment's hesitation, I said, "Yes, I'll do it."

So on September 15, 1979, I took off in an Air France plane for Paris. There was no one with me—no agent, no manager, no production assistant, and no Florence. My only companion was a small Sanyo cassette tape recorder I had just bought in Los Angeles. I figured that if I had so much trouble talking to people, it might be easier talking to a machine.

As my taxi took me into Paris from Orly airport, I marveled at the beauties of the city. I realized that though I had been to Paris on previous trips, I had never really seen it before. I always had arrived drunk, stoned, or both. I thought wryly that if you're an alcoholic-addict, it doesn't really matter what city you're in. You just want to get to your hotel and hit the bottle. It's safer and easier to stay home and do the same thing.

There was a reservation for me at the Raphael. It was a beautiful suite in one of the most luxurious hotels in Europe, but it didn't suit my purposes. The cast was staying there; other English people and Americans were there. I wanted to be in an environment where I'd be forced to confront only myself.

Not having to go to work right away, I wandered around in the charming streets near the Arc de Triomphe, and finally came across the little Hotel Victor Hugo in the Rue Copernic. I knew the word *chambre* (room) and somehow I made the receptionist understand that I might be interested in renting one for a long period of time. He took me up to the eighth floor, and there, just under the eaves, was one of the most delightful little suites I had ever seen. The ceiling was gabled. The windows looked out over the roofs of Paris. Pigeons were cooing on the sills. I had found my home away from home.

The director, Piers Haggart, was annoyed when I moved out of the Raphael. He's one of those British directors who likes to keep firm control over his cast. In fact, Piers was annoyed with me altogether. On the set, I felt the creativity beginning to stir in me again and I suggested little things that might juice up my part. I was playing a 1930s FBI man working with a British detective (Peter Sellers) on the trail of the nefarious Fu Manchu (also played by Sellers).

I'd say things to the director like, "Why must an FBI man always be Irish? Why can't I be Italian, and my name is Capone? I'm Al Capone's brother." Haggart would look at me stonily and say, "It's not in the script." I'd say, "Oh. I wasn't aware that this script is like the Torah, not a word can be changed or interpreted, not even by Maimonides." Haggart didn't know what I was talking about and Peter Sellers didn't care; he was ill. It wasn't too long before he had the massive heart attack that killed him.

So after a while, I gave up. I just went to work at the Boulogne Studio whenever I was needed, which wasn't very often, and I did my lines as written—and I looked forward to my evenings and days off in my wonderful little attic on the Rue Copernic.

On the morning of September 22, 1979, one week after I had arrived, I pulled out my cassette recorder and began a long series of daily conversations with myself. I was very self-conscious at first. For example, I had to have the radio on, playing music, before I could start talking. But even on that first day of taping, I realized I was doing a very interesting thing. I had split myself into two personalities, and I was Sid talking to Sidney. I wasn't aware of it until later, when I played those tapes over and over again, but, as Sid, I was using many of the techniques that had subliminally lodged in my mind from all the hours I had spent with psychiatrists.

In that first tape, I said, "Well, Sidney, here we are all alone—just the two of us. We're going to have a lot of time together because neither of us speaks French and there's nobody else to talk to. We can talk to the cast, but that's not going to do us any good because we've got to make friends with each other. We're going to be together twenty-four hours a day. And if *I'm* not going to have any fun, *you're* not going to have any fun."

And so it started. I'd talk to the tape recorder when I woke up in the morning, I'd talk when I got home in the evening, and sometimes I'd have a third conversation between Sid and Sidney before I went to bed. I'm an audio person. I get more out of listening than reading. So when I played back the tapes, I could see the changes in me, the swings in mood between morning and night of the same day. Gradually the understanding came to me that I was in a good routine—that nobody is happy or sad all the time. If you are, something is wrong. You must have balance. And balance was what was lacking in my life.

In the meantime, I also found that I was having some fascinating discussions with Sidney. I'd plead with him, argue with him, even have terrible fights with him. Here are some representative examples, transcribed verbatim from my Paris tapes, tentative at first:

You're getting mad because this tape machine isn't working right. Don't get mad. Learn how to work things, Sidney, *please.* . . . It's all right to believe in luck, Sidney, but astrology, like they were talking about it on the set today, is out. Astronomy, yes. Astrology, no. What does Saturn have to do with your taking a shit? . . . Sidney, you've got to make a better connection between your brain and your tongue and your lips. Your diction is terrible. . . . You're going to be something you always wanted to be—someone you could be proud of. Right now, you're not so proud. You've got to have strength; my God, you need strength. Your brain, that's where you need the strength. Now you're finding out where you are *half* the time. If you could only get to the other half. You're a lonely man, but you're only lonely because you make yourself lonely. You're like Samson. They've cut off your hair and you don't know who you are. So start finding out. The only way to find out is by this method. Talking, playing it back, listening—with nobody else here.

On the third day, I had a real knock-down-drag-out with Sidney:

Well, so you want to take a drink? Let's talk about it. How about a nice good drink? You'll forget everything, heh? Then you'll think you're not responsible because then you're a little baby and they'll have to take care of you, right? You're a little baby and not responsible, and you can get angry and do terrible things. Did it ever occur to you that you use up the same energy being angry as you do being happy? So do you think it's worth going through all this, with that boozing you have in mind? You say yeah, Sidney? Well, you're wrong. I went through it and it stinks. So you're wrong, Sidney, outright wrong. You idiot! You stupid shmuck! Why the hell are you even thinking like this?

Early on, we got into the subject of anger:

The first thing to do is to be happy, Sidney. Let yourself enjoy a meal. Let yourself enjoy a cigar. Let yourself alone. If that taxi driver yelled something at you, so what? Is it worth getting in a fight with him and maybe busting a knuckle? And so what if that stagehand took your chair away at the studio today? There are plenty of chairs, so the worst that happens is that you sit in a chair that doesn't have your name on it. Does your ass know the difference? Is it worth eating yourself up and letting it spoil your whole day? I'm telling you, Sidney, I really don't need this. I'm not taking this from you anymore. So shove it.

We talked a lot about guilt and how it tied in with lack of self-esteem:

You know what you used to do, Sidney? You drank because you felt guilty and then you felt even more guilty because you drank. It all feeds on itself. And what did you feel guilty about in the first place? Because you were doing better than your father? Bullshit. Your father did the best he could with the conditions of his life, and you did the best you could with the conditions of *your* life. It wasn't your *fault*. You made your own luck. . . . And let's analyze this other bullshit about how you were unworthy of your success and some Power took it away from you. Let me ask you something, Sidney. Your greatest hero in the whole world was Albert Einstein, right? So how about when his secretary phoned you at the studio that day in 1955 and said Dr. Einstein wanted you to visit him at his home in Princeton? Do you remember how you rushed out to read books on his theory of Relativity, and how you never saw him because he died suddenly that Saturday? And how about what Dr. Oppenheimer told you later: that the great Einstein was such a fan of yours that he wanted to include you in his studies of the Human Equation? For God's sake,

Sidney, if that doesn't make you feel worthy and build up your self-esteem, what could? *You* made Einstein aware of you, Sidney. You and you alone. So I don't want to hear any more of this bullshit about how unworthy you were. . . .

We kept coming back to the subject of booze:

With drinking, Sidney, the whole thing is a state of mind. Do you like the taste? No. Do you really feel you can't do without it? No. There are guys who tell you, "I had my last drink on Wednesday, March 2, at 3:19 P.M." Then you know that guy is going to drink again because he devotes so much energy to keeping track. You don't do that, Sidney, because you're finally learning that you're allergic to alcohol. For you, it's poison. That's it. Keep it up. It's a good sign that you're maturing and don't want to be a little baby anymore. The A.A. people keep track. That's their method and anything that works I don't knock. It's good. If you climb up in a tree and bang two pots together and it makes you stop drinking, it's good. And for you, what you're doing is working—so it's good.

Another time, we tied in drinking, anger, and suicide:

Sidney, you should realize something about your anger. When you drove your car, you almost *wanted* to be in an accident. It was part of the suicide game you were playing. You wanted to see how fast, how close you could come. Again, you were the child, seeing how much you could get away with. And there was the attraction that maybe it was going to work some day and you'd be dead. . . . If some other car cut you off, you got crazy. You had to get even.

How dare he cut you off, so now you're going to speed up even more and cut *him* off. How could you be so fuckin' dumb, Sidney? You cut him off and it gives you pleasure? No. You'd still be mad when you got home, so you'd start yelling at Florence. For what? What a waste of time. What did it gain you? Getting even is the biggest waste of time in life. You could have driven nice and quiet, and nothing would have happened to you, and you would have been happy, and Florence would have been happy. That's the way you gotta keep thinking, Sidney.

We discussed the family quite a bit:

You alway had the excuse: "Look at the pressure I'm under. Look at all I'm doing. So why should I worry if Florence is having a good time or not? She's got it good. Look at all the money she has." And all that time she didn't have it so good, shielding you from yourself, shielding the kids from you. "Go to bed, Daddy's sick," she used to say to them. And how many times did you push the kids away when they were reaching out to you? When Rick was a little boy, he wanted to play baseball with you, he tried to play Ping-Pong with you. And what was your excuse? "Look at the pressure I'm under." Bullshit, Sidney. You wanted to keep being the child yourself and didn't want to take responsibility for your own life.

I don't want to give the impression that I did nothing but talk to myself during those five months in Paris. For one thing, I kept up the physical exercise. I worked out in my room every morning before breakfast. I even used my fractured French to try to buy barbells in a sporting goods store, but

232

when the clerk came out with a hockey puck, I gave up and stuck to sit-ups and push-ups.

Rain or shine, I walked miles nearly every day. I couldn't get over the magnificence of this city I never really had seen before. I'd walk to L'Etoile, down the Champs-Elysées to the Place de la Concorde, and finally to the Tuileries Gardens— drinking it all in, smelling the flowers. I must have trudged miles along the banks of the Seine, watching the Bateaux-mouches and the other river traffic.

Occasionally, I had dinner with people from the cast and crew of the picture. It wasn't too stimulating because a lot of them were getting smashed and I wasn't. I got bored. I noticed for the first time how people tend to keep repeating themselves when they're drunk. I wondered about how many times I was guilty of that without realizing it.

I had dinner with Peter Sellers only once. We had a lot in common, but we strangely found little to talk about. Peter obviously was ill and distracted. He was about to fire Piers Haggart and take over the directing himself. It was to become a terrible burden for a man in his state of health. The only time he got animated was when, hunting around for a subject that might interest him, I mentioned Spike Jones's orchestra and the crazy Marx Brothers-type things they used to do on the stage. It turned out that Peter, with his wild inventive mind, had been a big fan of Spike Jones.

It was indirectly through Peter that I noticed one of my first signs of improvement, in my tapes. He was directing the picture by now and he called me in one day. I had a big scene coming up. He asked me if I minded if he changed the script so that another actor named Steve Franken could do it instead of me. Sellers said, "Sid, you've already had a big solo in this film, speaking in musical terms, and Steve has had none. So let Steve take this scene. You've *had* the adulation of the world."

I said, "No, that was one period of my life. I've been sick and now I'm going on to another period. I'm still on my way to getting well. I want you to know that. But it's OK with me if Steve does the scene."

That night I had the following interesting conversation with Sidney on my tape machine:

Well, Sidney, I'm proud of you. You were upset, but you didn't let it throw you completely, like in the old days. It's one of the things you've learned to cope with. You like yourself now, so other people, Sellers and Franken, like *you*. Sidney, what you have learned! What a great experience! God, what you've learned. Put it to use.

Later, there was another promising sign. The producer, Zev Braun, got a print of *Ten from Your Show of Shows*, and he screened it one rainy Sunday afternoon for the cast and crew. The screening was in a restaurant where Americans hung out. There were several young American college kids there who played for French basketball teams, and they watched, too. I half looked at the screen and I half kept looking at David Tomlinson, a fine British actor I greatly admired. Dave laughed, and his mouth hung open, and when it was over, he came up and wrung my hand, saying that now he understood my reputation. The other people clapped and cheered.

My tape that night was like a song of joy:

That was *you*, Sidney. Nobody else. No Power. It was *you*. Look what you have to work with. Look what you can draw on. Yes. Energy. Good, sharp, clean timing. That's what you have to work with. It takes a little more concentration, but you can do it. Marvelous. Kids laughed and they'd never heard of me. David Tomlinson's mouth was hanging open. My God, it gives you confidence to finally realize it was *you* who did it. Put it to good use, Sidney. Don't throw it away. The main thing is to keep doing it, Sidney. Don't let up. You've learned how to think.

And then, much later, this important tape:

So you finally called Steve Allen to thank him for the nice things he wrote about you. That's just the beginning, because you've got a lot of people to thank, Sidney. You thought you were sensitive, but you weren't, which is why you never realized that people were for you; they weren't against you. You were fighting *yourself*. You understand that now. You have friends. People care. So here's your chance, Sidney. Show them that by taking care of yourself, by liking yourself, you're liking them. You have to have friends, Sidney. You have to have people who will inspire. You can't live by yourself; you can't live in your own world. That's crazy. Learn how to be a friend.

As I said before, I didn't know what I was doing by talking to myself on these tapes in Paris (a procedure, by the way, which I still use every day). All I cared about was that I was getting better, that I was making friends with myself—and the world. I was functioning. I was happy—at least part of the time. My confidence had returned.

It was another two years before I learned that there was a solid scientific basis for the technique I thought I had just haphazardly improvised. I described my technique in detail to Scott Leith, one of the skilled counselor-therapists at the Chemical Dependency Center of St. John's Hospital in Santa Monica, California. He has specialized in alcoholism therapy for years, dealing with patients ranging from Skid Row bums to multimillionaire corporate heads; and the St. John's C.D.C. is among the nation's best.

## Scott Leith

*Mr. Caesar's experience is not unusual for people who have previously gone through a lot of therapies unsuccessfully. In dealing with the self, they are subconsciously using elements of all those therapies they once rejected.*

*From what I know of Mr. Caesar's case, and after having discussed it with him, it is a phenomenon akin to spontaneous Jungian analysis. To Jung, the unconscious and the spiritual were the same. In Canada, Mr. Caesar obviously had a spiritual experience. It has happened with other alcoholics and addicts I have known. It always comes after a period in which the patient is in the depths of despair. Then he says to himself, in effect, "The devil is dead. It's had its way with me. Now it's given up on me and will leave me alone."*

*In Paris, by talking into his tape machine, Mr. Caesar also was following the Jungian theory. Part of a therapy is having a dialogue with that part of you which is the source of the anger and the pain, and coming to an accommodation with it. Basically, it's acceptance of self, "making friends with yourself," as he puts it.*

*In a sense, Mr. Caesar successfully split himself in two, in order to accomplish this. In "Sid," he became his own parent. In "Sidney," the self-destructive segment of him, he was the wayward child.*

*Every therapy is a continuing process, but it is working when the parent continues to tame the wayward child.*

# 26

# Flowers for Florence

I hadn't been in Paris more than a month when my program for controlling the wayward child in me was put to the most crucial of tests. Florence phoned from California and said she was coming to Paris to spend a couple of weeks with me.

I was both excited and frightened at the prospect. I had been calling her and trying to explain what I was doing with my tape machine, but I knew she was still skeptical. Not that I could blame her. She had seen me through brief periods of improvement before, and I had always slipped back. Obviously, the Thanksgiving Day flap was still on her mind. Also, I hadn't been very good at explaining just what it was that I was up to with Sid talking to Sidney on the cassettes. Not knowing what Scott Leith told me much later, it was difficult to explain to *anyone*—without making them think I had flipped out and wasn't exactly playing with a full deck.

Florence arrived on a Wednesday. As luck would have it, this was the one day in nearly a week that I was badly needed at the studio. They were shooting one of my key scenes with Peter. There was nothing to do but send a car and driver out to the airport to pick her up and take her to my suite at the Hotel Victor Hugo. A bad start. I brooded about it all day.

We finally finished work at the studio at about six o'clock. A studio chauffeur drove me home, but we ran into the world's greatest daily traffic jam—the ten-lane automotive nightmare that occurs between six and seven around L'Etoile and the Arc de Triomphe. After moving only about fifty feet in twenty minutes, I got out and walked the rest of the way.

I rushed down the Avenue Kleber and passed one of the many flower-selling kiosks you see sprinkled all over Paris. I came to a sliding stop. I told the flower-lady to make up a bouquet of everything she had—asters, zinnias, chrysanthemums. The bouquet cost one hundred francs (about twenty-five dollars), probably the biggest sale she had made all day. As she carefully wrapped the bouquet, I thought of how little flowers ever had meant to me—until Paris. I also realized, quite painfully, that it probably was twenty-five years since I had personally selected and given flowers to Florence. For years, I had just told my secretary, "Call the florist and send something over to my wife."

When I got to the hotel, the reception desk was in a flurry of excitement. "Madame is here, in the suite," the concierge told me, and then everyone ran around to find a vase that would be suitable for the bouquet I had bought. As I knew by then, the French love anyone who loves flowers.

I finally got to the suite, followed by a maid carrying the

vase filled with flowers. Florence kissed me and then stared at the flowers. "I just bought these for you—myself," I said, nervously going into a routine about the heart of Paris being its year-round bounty of blossoms.

"Well, I'll be damned," Florence said, still staring at the flowers.

And so we did finally get off to a good start, even though Florence's skepticism didn't immediately disappear. I couldn't wait to show her "my city," newly found for me but more familiar to her from our previous visits. On my days off, we walked. We went to the Tuileries, to the Louvre, to the Cathedral of Notre Dame, walking all the way home along the banks of the Seine. Florence had had a foot operation, and I carried extra pairs of comfortable shoes for her in a paper bag, so she could change into them whenever she wanted to. She kept staring at the bag of shoes the way she had stared at the bouquet of flowers. She couldn't believe it.

I don't think she really believed until one night when circumstances put me to a severe test. We went to the movies. It was a little theater on the Champs-Elysées, and I still remember the picture we saw. It was Francis Ford Coppola's *Apocalypse Now*, which we had missed in the United States.

When we got out of the theater, it was pouring rain outside, and I had a regression. I reverted to the old Sid. When I couldn't get a cab, I began cursing and screaming, as if the weather and the taxi drivers were teaming up against me, personally. Florence said, "It's not so terrible. Let's walk back to the hotel." I said, "You want to walk in the rain? All right. That's it. I'll show you walking in the rain." And I strode off, down the Champs-Elysées.

When I turned around, Florence was gone. I ran around in the downpour looking for her. Maybe she had popped into

Le Drug Store? No, she wasn't there. Maybe she was standing in one of the shop entrances. I checked them all in that block. No Florence. Finally, I guessed she was so angry with me that she had just taken off down one of the side streets and gone back to the hotel. I rushed to the hotel. I was right.

When I walked into the suite, I said, "Oh, there you are, Florence." She glowered at me and didn't answer. Then I calmly went into the bathroom and toweled myself off. I removed my soaked clothes and put on dry ones.

When I came out, I said, "You see? You walk in the rain, so what's the worst that can happen? You get wet. So you dry yourself off, and you don't let it spoil your whole evening. That's the way I think now. That's the new me. So now, my darling, let's go down to that Chinese restaurant you like so much, La Belle Chine, and we'll have a nice, pleasant dinner."

Florence was stunned. My usual pattern in such a situation was to holler, and start a big fight that would go on for hours, blaming Florence for everything—including the rain. She was still unconvinced. "And what if it's still raining?" she asked cautiously.

I said, "If it's still raining when we finish dinner, we'll come back to the hotel. If the rain has stopped, we'll take a nice long walk. Paris is never more beautiful than after a rain."

"Well, OK," Florence said.

We had a lovely dinner and a marvelous walk afterward. All in all, it turned out to be one of the most pleasant evenings we'd had together since we were kids in the Catskills.

Florence was supposed to go back to Los Angeles that Friday. It was the end of the usual two-week visit I'm sure she had always looked on as being part of her duty. But on Thursday she said she'd kind of like to stay on a little longer. She ended up staying on for more than six weeks.

241

Where Have I Been?

We did everything together. We toured Versailles, and when the film company moved to St. Gervais in the French Alps for location filming, Florence went with me. The weather was miserable; storms raged around Mont Blanc. Everyone was complaining about the rain and sleet—but not us. We were having a wonderful time.

When we returned to Paris, Rick joined us for a few days. He'd been doing some medical work in Scotland. Florence, always trying to patch things up between us, had told him how different I was and that it might be a good idea for him to come over to see for himself.

I'm not a sentimental man, but I nearly broke down when Rick walked in. It was the first time we'd really talked since our blow-up on Thanksgiving Day the year before. Rick was still wary, but we made a good start toward being friends again. I told him about my tapes and even played some of them for him. He was very interested because he had worked in a psychiatric hospital and he was considering psychiatry as a field in which he might specialize. He made me feel good when he said, "Dad, you may not know it, but you've been making some progress over the last ten years—even with your two steps forward and one step backward."

"No more steps backward," I said.

"I hope so," he said.

With Rick gone, I had another two weeks alone with Florence. I didn't talk to my tape recorder as much when she was there because that was a private thing between Sid and Sidney. She did hear me occasionally, though, and while she didn't really understand the entire concept of what I was doing, she understood enough.

La Belle Chine, just down the street from the hotel on the Rue Copernic, continued to be our favorite restaurant. We ate there nearly every night. I had learned that it's no different ordering Chinese food from a non-French-speaking Chinese waiter than ordering Chinese food from a non-English-speaking Chinese waiter. Words like "egg roll" and "lemon chicken" make up an international language of their own.

La Belle Chine is far from being the most chic restaurant in Paris, which is why I was amazed one night when I looked across at the next table and saw what I thought was a familiar face.

I said to Florence, "Could that be Dr. Jonas Salk?"

She said, "Of the Salk polio vaccine?"

I said, "Yes. And that woman with him. Seems to be his wife. She used to be . . ."

Florence broke in, "Picasso's lady, Françoise Gilot, and a very fine artist herself. But I don't think that's who they are."

"Oh," I said.

We finished our dinner and took a walk over to the Champs-Elysées and back. When we passed the restaurant again, the couple was just coming out.

This time I couldn't stand it. I ran after the man and said, "Excuse me, sir, but are you Jonas Salk?"

He said, "Yes, I am. But I couldn't help noticing you in the restaurant. Are *you* Sid Caesar?"

We talked for a while and made arrangements to see each other again at La Belle Chine. I couldn't wait to get up to the suite—and my cassette recorder. This is the conversation I had with myself that night.

Sidney, you shmuck, what did I tell you about your self-worth. Remember how we talked about Albert Einstein being one of your biggest fans? Tonight you meet a man

243

who is one of the greatest medical minds in the whole world. You're in awe of him and afraid to approach him, and he's in awe of *you* and afraid to approach you. Self-worth, Sidney. Keep that in mind the next time you feel that you're nothing. Keep in mind that the great Jonas Salk doesn't think you're nothing. Good-night, Sidney. Sleep well.

From the next room, Florence asked, "What are you doing, Sid?"

"Not much," I said, "just talking to myself."

The following week Florence went back to California, and I had another two-and-a-half months of just talking to myself.

# 27
# Enjoying Myself Enjoying Myself

My work on the film was finished on February 2, and I left Paris for home on February 5, 1980. I had been there since September. It had been the most important five-and-a-half months of my life—including the Glory Days of "Your Show of Shows" and "Caesar's Hour."

A few days before I departed for California, I had a very strange and exhilarating experience. I'm a superstitious man who believes in symbols. This one really got to me.

It was dusk, about four-thirty in the afternoon in Paris at that time of the year. I had taken my daily walk to the Tuileries

Gardens. At the very instant I turned to walk back to my hotel, I saw an incredible sight that I've never encountered before or since. In the split second I turned, all the streetlights went on, down the Champs-Elysées, on the Arc de Triomphe, and beyond, in all directions, as far as the eye could see. It was a breathtaking sight, as if all the fireflies of the world had suddenly congregated in one place. In all the months I had been in Paris, I had never been in the right place at the exact right time to view this amazing spectacle. And it never happened again.

I drank it in for a few minutes. Then I went back to the hotel. I picked up my cassette recorder (by now, I had replaced the Sanyo with a more sophisticated Toshiba), and I said:

Well, Sidney, now you know what it means when they say Paris is the City of Lights. Boy-oh-boy-oh-boy. Have you ever seen anything like that in your life? And how about what it means for *you* symbolically, Sidney? It means that the lights have gone on for you, too. Why else did you see it from that specific spot in that specific millionth of a second? It's a sign. Keep up the good work, Sidney. Keep remembering what you've learned here. And let's see about the turning on of the lights when you get back to Los Angeles.

It was indeed a portent. I had barely settled in at home in Beverly Hills, and had barely said hello to Florence, Karen, Maranee, and my dogs, Conus and Sascha, when the phone rang. It was my agent, Tom Korman. NBC wanted me not for one but for *two* TV series, both of which would begin in March.

Neither of the series was what you would call a world-beater, and neither of them lasted very long, but they got me back in the arena where I belonged. I was given a chance to be funny in my own style, and, most important of all, I was allowed to *contribute* creatively. I hadn't been permitted to do that for a long, long time. I hadn't been capable of it for a long, long time either.

The first of the two series was "The Big Show," an hour-and-a-half variety program that NBC President Fred Silverman thought would re-create the production values and excitement of Max Liebman's "spectaculars" in the old days. Nick Vanoff was the producer. There was a rink for ice-skating ballets and a pool for water ballets. Overall, it didn't work, but Vanoff gave me a chance to team with one of the all-time television talents, Steve Allen.

I don't know if Steve knew what I had gone through, but he couldn't have been more marvelous to me. He said, "Sid, we've got to come up with some funny skits, so I want you to sit in with me and the writers, just like you used to do."

What a tonic that was for me, tossing ideas back and forth the way I once had with Doc Simon, Mel Brooks, Larry Gelbart, and the others. For example, someone came up with the idea of spoofing the then-popular Irish Spring soap commercial, in which a variety of strong-smelling Irish athletes, having just played soccer and such, become socially acceptable to their girls again after showering with the soap. I contributed a lot of ideas to that skit, which was one of those most liked by the critics in the short history of the show. My best suggestion: when I rush forward to greet my girl, played by the wonderful young comedienne Mimi Kennedy, not only does my pungency cause her to faint, but all the surrounding trees also fall down.

In another fine skit, Steve wanted to satirize the reporting techniques of "60 Minutes." We and the writers had a ball

247

developing *that* one. Steve played a Mike Wallace type, and I was the object of his investigation—a crook who had pulled off every conceivable type of scam. Steve kept interviewing me, and I'd innocently and reasonably deny everything. After each discussion of a specific case of my wrongdoing, however, he'd run a film, shot clandestinely, showing how I had done exactly what I denied. I was in an alley selling stolen jewelry, counting money, drinking champagne; I was filmed paying bribe money; and so on. It was a lot like the "Caesar's Hour" sketches. I played a big part in developing it, and I felt very good doing it.

While I was doing two of "The Big Show" extravaganzas with Steve, I was also costarring in three of the six aired segments of "Pink Lady." This show was another of Fred Silverman's big mistakes, but once again it gave me a chance to get back into action and exercise my long-unused creativity. It was like going to a gym for my mind.

Pink Lady was the name of a singing team of two very pretty Japanese young ladies. The problem was that though they sang in English (apparently they had learned the words phonetically), they spoke only Japanese. They needed an interpreter just to say "hello" to me when I showed up. Rudy DeLuca, the director, was frantic. He said to me, "We've got to come up with comedy skits for these girls. They just can't sing for the whole show. How the fuck can we do skits when they don't speak English? Apparently Silverman thought they could learn the words of the skits like they learned the words of the songs. But who's got the time to do that? And what about their reactions, their timing, when they won't know what the fuck they're saying?" He was so mad he was ready to quit.

I knew Rudy from when he was one of Mel Brooks's writers, and I calmed him down. I said, "Leave it to me."

He said, "How can I leave it to you when we have here one of the world's greatest examples of failure to communicate."

I said, "Cool it, Rudy. What we'll do here is the Jewish-father jokes, but the father will be Japanese and so will his two daughters."

He said, "But you don't speak Japanese, and neither does our audience."

I said, "You never heard my Japanese double-talk? Who will know? And I'll throw in enough Kabuki technique so the girls will get the drift of what I'm saying and they'll follow along."

I've never tackled anything so difficult, but it worked. Rudy and I helped with the scripts. We first came up with the idea that I was a very strict, traditional Japanese father. The two girls were dressed in kimonos that covered them from neck to ankle, but I'd scream and yell at them—in my Japanese double-talk, but with an occasional English word thrown in: "Your neck is showing. The tips of your toes are showing. You're shameless. You're harlots."

As I pointed at those parts of their anatomy and yelled, the girls got the drift of what I was saying and they *did* follow along with their reactions and answers in real Japanese. Apparently, I had struck a familiar chord with them. Maybe they had experienced the same situation with a strict father at home. Anyway, it worked. Thank God. What else could you do with them?

The first skit led to others, in which the girls were courted by young men. As the father, I kept close track of the courting time. I had a gong and an hourglass. I hit the gong when the courting was to begin. Then, when the sand had run down in the hourglass, I hit the gong again. "Courting is over." The audience didn't have to understand what I was saying, but by my actions in hustling the young men out, my meaning was clear. This skit, fortunately, required very little dialogue.

The progression of sketches led up to a wedding. Again, it was more pantomime than dialogue, and it was very effective. Like fathers everywhere, I was appalled at the costs of the reception, and I kept track of the tab—but with an abacus. I demanded an accounting of each portion of food served, and sent back each portion that was not going to be eaten— except for one which I magnanimously sent over to the conductor of the orchestra.

When it came time to cut the wedding cake, I hacked it up furiously with a samurai sword. This got the biggest laugh of the entire series from the studio audience. Younger television viewers have the idea that the Berserk Samurai was invented by John Belushi and "Saturday Night Live." They don't realize that before many of them were born, Carl Reiner and I first used these same *shtick* on "Your Show of Shows."

With NBC wallowing in failures in 1980, "Pink Lady" finished out its six shows and was canceled. It was, however, an important learning experience for me in reestablishing my strengths—after so many years of coping with my real and imagined weaknesses.

It continued to be a good year. I worked almost constantly because I *wanted* to work. I hadn't felt that way in a long, long time.

Right after "Pink Lady," Mel Brooks called. He was doing his film *The History of the World, Part One*, and he wanted me to play the head caveman in the prehistoric sequence of the picture. He sent me a script. I read it and went over to see him. It was like old times. Mel and I immediately started fighting, although now the roles were reversed. When I wanted to make some changes to improve the caveman sequence, he said, "It's my script and nobody is going to change a word in it." We yelled back and forth, just like in our early days together, and finally he agreed that my suggestions had some merit. He ended up grinning at me and saying, "At least this fighting is better than *Silent Movie*, when you walked through the picture like a zombie."

My suggestions were comparatively minor ones, but they helped. In a fire-making scene, I made a big thing of heating a stone in the flame of a torch and then trying to ignite some straw by placing the hot rock in it. Of course it didn't work. I never thought of the obvious method of simply lighting the straw with the torch. In another scene, I created the world's first choir by dropping rocks on the feet of my fellow cavemen, causing them all to howl in unison.

When my sequence in Mel's film was finished, again there was another interesting role waiting for me. I had hardly had time to catch my breath since Paris, but for the first time in years, that's the way I wanted it. So I signed to do a stage revival of Cole Porter's 1934 Broadway musical *Anything Goes*. My costar was to be Ginger Rogers.

In the original Broadway cast, the female lead was Ethel Merman. It was the role that made her. She sang those wonderful Cole Porter songs like "Anything Goes" and "I Get a Kick Out of You," and even though the plot was crazy and old-fashioned, she was ably supported by William Gaxton, playing a gangster, and his sidekick, Victor Moore. In the later Paramount movie, the leads were Mitzi Gaynor, Bing Crosby, and Donald O'Connor. In our 1980 version it was Ginger Rogers, Ross Petty, and me. I was the Victor Moore–Donald O'Connor sidekick character.

I was in awe of Ginger when we started rehearsals. She's still absolutely beautiful, and very talented. I learned a lot from her. When we first met, I was delighted to find out that she had a lot of respect for me, too.

I said, "At least I won't have to dance the Continental with you."

She replied, "And at least I won't have to do a silent movie with *you*."

So we got off on a good footing, and it remained that way throughout the production.

My biggest challenge was to enhance my part, which was comparatively small in the original Broadway show. As written, my biggest moment would come when I sang and danced "Friendship" in a trio with Ginger and Ross Petty. You know the song: "Friendship, friendship, it's a perfect blendship . . . When other friendships they are forgot, ours will still be hot." With Ginger coaching me and helping me with this number, how could I go wrong?

The problem was with the story line. If you remember the corny old plot, the gangster and his sidekick are "on the lam" when they join up with the girl. There isn't much sense to what happens, except that Cole Porter wrote it for William Gaxton to have all the good lines. Poor Victor Moore mostly tagged along, dressed as a priest with a machine gun under his cassock.

Without stepping on anyone's toes, I began to gradually add to the sidekick part. Nobody seemed to mind because it improved the story by today's standards. I worried about Cole Porter spinning in his grave, but I figured that if he were alive today, he might have gotten a few laughs out of what I did. For example, there's a scene in which the gangster and his sidekick entice two Chinese gentlemen into a game of strip poker. The idea is to obtain their Oriental clothing as a disguise. The scene is pretty funny in itself, but I milked it for minutes longer with every card-cheating routine I could think of. Another example: Roxy (Ginger Rogers) comes onstage disguised as a Chinese maiden. Adding to the scene, I auctioned her off—conducting the auction in four languages. I was like a carpenter, adding to the structure nail by nail, board by board.

The show opened on the road in Kansas City, where we got quite good reviews, and then we went on to do fourteen more weeks in fourteen cities. We ended up at the Wilshire Theater in Los Angeles. Poor Ginger. The critics were very catty about her, though they were very nice to me. I personally thought Ginger was sensational, in a very difficult, outdated role. I often wish the critics would take such factors into consideration.

Anyway, I was home for Christmas and I was feeling very good about myself. I said to Florence, "Let's have a party. A great big party for all our old friends. Right here in this house."

She looked at me as if I had sprung a leak. She said, "We haven't had a big party in over twenty years."

I said, "So, OK. So it's about time."

We had the party on December 12, 1980. Nearly everyone came. Neil Simon was there with his wife, Marsha Mason; Mel Brooks with his wife, Anne Bancroft; the Larry Gelbarts; the Carl Reiners; the Mel Tolkins; Nanette Fabray; Buddy Hackett; Jan Murray; Jack Carter; Dick Martin; and dozens more.

Where Have I Been?

At first, I guess, I wanted to have the party just to see who would show up. When the guests had arrived, however, I realized that I had a deeper motivation. It was a test. With all that booze flowing in a natural social environment, would I want to have a drink? I was never tempted—not even once. The craving, the need, was totally gone. Then again, I wanted to see if I could enjoy myself just enjoying myself. I did. It was a wonderful evening, filled with wonderful conversation. There was no small talk. No "It's a nice day and how do you think tomorrow will be," or "Those are nice shoes," or "Hey, did you see so-and-so, and what's he doing now?" It was all serious, intelligent conversation that lasted late into the night. It all was a revelation to me. In the old days, when I was drunk, I *thought* I was enjoying myself. This night I enjoyed myself simply because I was important to *me*, not to anybody else. My creative juices were flowing. I was a participant in the discussions and holding my own very well.

The only person at the party who mentioned my previous condition was Larry Gelbart, a man with enormous insight. He said, "Hey, you look fantastic, great. And your state of mind—I haven't seen you as vital as this in years. For a while, I was afraid you were locking yourself up here like Norma Desmond in *Sunset Boulevard* looking at her old films over and over again."

The party didn't break up until about 4:00 A.M. Florence hugged me and told me how proud she was at the way I had handled myself. Maranee said it was the best party she had ever seen. Karen was so excited, not only about me, but about all the photos she had taken of the celebrities. After all, she was only twenty-three, and having grown up in my Dark Period, she had never before seen me with all these talented people—with whom I once had been so close.

Before going to bed that night, I went into my study and found my cassette recorder. I turned it on and had a long conversation with Sidney.

OK, Sidney, this is December 12, 1980. Do you remember how you were just two-and-a-half years ago, in 1978? You were locked away in your room, in bed. You were afraid to come out. You thought only of death. And now, look at the difference in you tonight. It's a turning point in your life. You found out tonight that you're important to yourself— that it's the only thing that should matter to you. Being important to *other* people is only relative. You were important to some people here tonight; you were not important to others. Who cares? What counts is that you now know that you *are* something. You felt good about yourself tonight, and, sort of by osmosis, your guests picked up that feeling, and they felt good about you again. Look how far you've come, Sidney—not only since 1978 but also since 1958. When you felt you had to be important to other people, it was a whole other thing: what kind of car you drove, what kind of clothes you wore, how much you would tip. It was all ego. What happened tonight was not ego. You didn't just enjoy yourself. You enjoyed yourself enjoying yourself. You're learning, Sidney. Keep on learning to be important to you and you alone. That's a learning process you can never let up on. It has to go on for the rest of your life.

# 28
# A Delayed Flower Child

After the party, I spent a lot of time at home. My family was still a little shy of me. It actually took them two years before they accepted that I was on the mend and wasn't just going through a phase.

Various things that I did got through to each of them in a different way. Rick, for example, eventually was won over by my completely changed attitude toward my surroundings.

In Paris I had found out about the beauties of nature for the first time. I had always thought of nature as something that was just there—like a backdrop on a TV stage. Now, I would stand on the patio at nightfall and watch the sunset until dusk had fallen. I'd talk about the various colors in the sky behind the Santa Monica Mountains and marvel at the changing combinations. Rick came down from Portland once and caught me doing that. He acted as if it was someone else's father, not his.

Then there were the flowers, which I had first learned to appreciate in Paris. We had never had more than a few geraniums in the backyard. Now I wanted color everywhere. I planted snapdragons, snow poppies, alyssum, zinnias, roses, azaleas, pansies, marigolds—everything I could get my hands on. I watered, weeded, cut bouquets for Florence. I think this is what finally got through to Rick. It was one of the many changes in me that he was totally unprepared for.

## Rick Caesar

*I've become aware that my father, from being an aggressive almost neo-Fascist-type American, has become what you could call the equivalent of a delayed flower child. I know that for some people, thinking back to the 1960s, the term has sort of a pejorative effect. But I don't mean it in that sense. I mean it in its most positive aspect: What's wrong with peace and love?*

*With Dad's new love of flowers, he's expressing his new self in both a literal and figurative way. He enjoys the beauty of flowers, but at the same time he's saying he wants to get along, that peace and harmony are more important than any individual issue, more important than being right, more important than showing off. To me, it means that you no longer have such a fear of revealing your weaknesses that you have to destroy your whole environment. Dad is able to relax for the first time and enjoy those things in his environment—including his family.*

*I must honestly say that if he had been this way when I*

*was growing up, my choice of profession might very well have been different. I probably* would *have become a writer—instead of selecting the one career that was most different from his.*

Karen first began to believe in the validity of my improvement for a totally different reason. My younger daughter is a great animal lover. Sometimes I think she likes dogs and cats better than she likes people.

When I got back from Paris, we had two dogs in the household—both of which are still very much part of it. There's Conus, a huge gentle Rottweiler, who was rescued from the pound by Rick. Then there's Sascha, a beautiful gray female Siberian husky, who was rescued from the pound by Shelly. As I recovered from my Dark Period, I became aware of these wonderful animals for the first time. I talked to them; I played with them; I learned their idiosyncrasies. Conus is the faithful, distinguished gentleman. Sascha is flighty, coquettish, a little neurotic, but capable of great love. Soon, I was taking them out for their daily walks—and enjoying it. Before that, only Karen, Florence, and Maranee did it.

That's what finally got through to Karen.

## Karen Caesar

*We had had dogs before. First, there was Julius, an enormous Great Dane. I think Dad bought him only because he wanted to have the biggest dog on the block, just like he always had to have the biggest car. Julius was a status symbol, a possession. Dad hardly ever paid any attention to him.*

*When Julius died, we got Cindy, who was half-collie and*

*half-shepherd. To Dad, she was just another prop around the house. She was terrified of him and spent most of her time in my room.*

*After he got back from Paris, I wasn't very impressed when Dad admired sunsets and puttered around with the flowers in the yard. I thought it was an act. I thought he was just trying to ingratiate himself with Mother—though even that would have been an improvement.*

*I finally became a true believer, I finally was able to accept the fact that he* had *changed, when I saw him treating Conus and Sascha like grandchildren. He was talking baby talk to them; he was playing with them; he was running out to get their favorite dog biscuits when there weren't any in the house.*

*That's when I came to think that at last there was a real father around, like everyone else's father.*

With Shelly, the acceptance of the changes in me was more grudging. Perhaps it was because, being the eldest, she had been around me longer than the others and had had more time to acquire her scars.

But, even with Shelly, there was a breakthrough. She came to me one day and said, "Dad, you and I never have had a father-daughter relationship. There are things I have to be able to discuss with you. We have to talk. We have to communicate."

It's still difficult for me to use the word "love," but I said to Shelly, "Sweetheart, I love you and I *want* to be able to talk to you. I'm going to try. At least we'll make a beginning. But you've got to realize that I've been sick for a long, long time, and I'm just learning to communicate with *myself.* I'll try."

Shelly accepted that. She laughed and said, "Well, I guess it *is* a beginning. At least you didn't brush me off and say, 'Go talk to your mother,' the way you used to."

Maranee was the pragmatist, as usual. She knew—as I did—that it was a matter of my holding on, one day at a time, even one hour at a time. When she watched me or heard me get through a particularly bad day or hour, I could see her looking at me approvingly out of those wise brown eyes, her face tipped forward.

Florence was the first to acknowledge that my new attitude wasn't temporary—or a fluke. That's because she was the principal beneficiary of it. I no longer indulged in that unreasonable squabbling with her. There were no more fights. I used to start a fight with her if she opened a door with her left hand instead of her right hand.

Why the fights? That was one of the first answers that came to me in my conversations with Sidney in Paris. It was all part of my pattern of punishing myself. I hollered at the kids to punish myself by repelling their love. I hollered at Florence and picked fights with her so I could punish myself by making it impossible for her to even consider having sex with me. Making love to Florence is one of the great pleasures of my life, so what better punishment than to act in such a way as to deprive myself of it.

Now that I knew I didn't *deserve* self-punishment, that I had done nothing wrong, that I had offended no Power, that there were many good reasons to like myself, that I did what I did because I didn't know any better—there no longer was any reason to fight with Florence and deprive myself of the love and support I needed.

In all aspects, my rehabilitation was a continuing process, taking positive steps to get through that one hour and one day at a time. Physically, I adhered religiously to my nutritious meat-free diet and kept improving my "mush" of yogurt, cereal, nuts, and fruits. I never missed a day of working out at home and going to the gym. I knew, from my medical reading, that it might take two years or more for my body to rid itself of the effects of the tons of destructive chemicals, alcohol and otherwise, that I had poured into it.

Mentally, I was learning to recognize the warning signals, the trigger mechanisms, that could set off my wild rages and destructive behavior. I was learning how to intercept the trigger before it could be pulled.

An old scenario with a new ending: I was driving to Whittier one night on a dark, narrow street. A car came up close behind me and the driver nearly blinded me by turning on his high-beam headlights. I pulled over to let him pass. Now I was behind him. An instinctive reaction from the old days caused me to flick on *my* high-beam headlights. He stopped his car, got out, and challenged me to fight. I could see he was smashed. Pre-Paris, I would have torn into him and beaten him to a pulp. Now I just said, "Sorry, Mac," and drove off. What a waste of time and energy just to get even with a total stranger who didn't mean a thing to me.

I had intercepted the trigger in myself before it could be pulled.

It wasn't that easy all the time.

Once, for example, I was called over to Paramount Studios to meet with two TV producers who had sold ABC a pilot for a new situation-comedy series. I was told they had been associated with "Taxi," a series I thought was quite good. Their new show was about a bar and the quaint characters who hung out in it. I was to be one of the quaint characters.

I had read the script, which they sent over to me in advance, and I didn't like it very much. The role they had in mind for me, in particular, was pure cardboard, strictly one-dimensional. But I saw some promise in it if I could be allowed to add some of my own *shtick*. So I went over to see the producers.

I expected to be meeting with Jim Brooks or Stan Daniels, two top talents, who, in addition to creating "Taxi," had previously been involved in "The Mary Tyler Moore Show," among others. Instead, I found myself in a room with a couple of twenty-five-year-olds who seemed to know of me only from a part I had played in the movie *Grease* in 1977. I soon realized that, like so many of their generation in the industry, their concept of comedy did not go back beyond "Gilligan's Island," on which they had been raised as children.

I said, "I have a few ideas to make my part a little more interesting and meaningful." They stared at me coldly and said, "We're perfectly satisfied with the part as we wrote it, Mr. Caesar." I felt my temper rising, but I controlled it. I went through the motions of having an amiable chat with them before I got up and said, "OK. That's it. Thank you. Good-bye." They were startled. Actors don't walk out on the almighty writer-producer when a possible five-year series contract is being dangled before them.

But I figured the concept was so poor it probably never would make it to a series anyway. Besides, even if it did, why would I want to be associated with such shit? In the old days, I would have blown my top in the kids' office. Then I would have brooded and sunk into a deep depression—and hit the bottle—over having been rejected.

Instead, I went home and sat on my patio, and looked at the flowers, and listened to a Mahler symphony on my radio. After that, I came up with an idea for a movie I'd like to do—a comic spoof of all the current "in" science fiction films—and I worked on it, in my head, for several hours. The degrading morning turned out to be a very creative afternoon. I was happy as a pissant when Florence finally called me in for dinner.

I kept developing my resources for controlling the trigger mechanism that sent me off into angers and depressions. Using aviation terms, I called it "being at the controls." When I felt myself slipping into rage or worry, even momentarily, I'd say to myself, "Hey, wait a minute. What is it that's upsetting you? Even if the worst happens, will it make your life any different from what it was this morning, or even a half hour ago?" And I would calm down. I was at the controls again.

But with people like me, recovery is an up-and-down thing. Sometimes you slip slightly and have to catch yourself. It happened when I changed agents—again. I still hadn't learned that agents are deal-makers, that mostly they can only sell properties when you yourself bring them in. I thought it would be different if I once again tried a large talent agency. It wasn't.

After the usual initial period of flirtation and courtship, I reached the point where my new agents wouldn't talk to me on the phone. They wouldn't return my calls. They wouldn't call me. I kept discussing this in the daily conversations I still had with myself, on my cassette recorder.

Well, Sidney, so the agents didn't call again. Nothing much is happening. That's all right, Sidney. Realize that and don't be crazy. Be patient, Sidney. Be patient. Keep control. You're the one who makes you happy; you're the one who makes you sad. It's so much easier to live when you keep remembering that.

After a while, I got mad—for a few minutes. But then I simply went back to Tom Korman, who always was glad to have me. I wrote a nice, polite "Letter of Dismissal" to the other agents. No rages. No going to their offices and smashing furniture. Nothing like the old days. It just happened that it didn't work out, so it didn't work out. My new philosophy.

I also developed a parallel philosophy during this period. It all began when I was on the road with Ginger Rogers in *Anything Goes*. I was reading one of my many books about Albert Einstein, and I came across a fascinating line by Hermann Minkowski, who had been Einstein's original physics teacher in Switzerland. Minkowski said, "If you want to put Einstein's theory of Relativity in one sentence, it would be: 'One man's now is another man's then.' "

That started me thinking along the following lines, various versions of which I have used on the stage:

While people keep waiting and waiting for something big to happen in life, the "now" is passing them by. Do you know how fast a "now" passes? At the rate of 186,000 miles per second, the speed of light. So no matter how much you love and enjoy a particular "now," that's how fast it becomes a "was." That "now" is never coming back, and that "was" ties into some "going-to-be." So if you don't learn from the "was's," you're going to have bad "going-to-be's," which completes the cycle by bringing in bad "nows." Thus, the only time you can switch around from a negative into a positive is in the "now." Because you *have* to do it now. You can't just *think* of doing it now because it rapidly becomes a "was," and it's too late. And "going-to-be" is you may do it and you may not. So if you do it now, you know it's done and you've got it. If you have a good "now," you have a good "was," which leads to a good "going-to-be." In other words, by taking advantage of a "now," maybe even changing a bad "now" into a good "now," you have a good "was," from which you can learn and change your whole cycle of life. That's why I never use the word "if" anymore. An "if" is a "never was."

Perhaps the English poets said the same thing better. Maybe it reads like gibberish. But when I rattle it off to audiences, they seem to grasp the meaning and they love it. Most important of all, the philosophy has been very valuable to me in my recovery. I don't let the "nows" go by anymore.

Even in my social life.

I used to dread going to parties. I am shy. I couldn't face up to the ritual of meeting new people. Today I look upon everyone I meet at a party as a potential "now," someone from whom I can learn something that can be a good "was" in my backlog of knowledge and experience. That's particularly true of women.

In the old days I used to talk only to the men at a party. That turned off some of my best friends, who had bright wives who didn't like being ignored by me. I have learned a lot since then.

At a recent Beverly Hills party, for example, I enjoyed a lot more pleasant "nows" in my conversations with the women than with the men. I comfortably discussed politics, economics, and world affairs with them. There was a woman surgeon, a rare book collector, a psychologist, an anthropologist. Florence eagerly joined the conversations, too. There was a time when she would just sit watching me puffing cigars and talking show business with men I already knew.

On our way home, we discussed how I had changed. I

said, "Just like with everything else in my life today, I've changed because, for the first time, I *wanted* to change. Once you make friends with yourself and you feel worthy enough to enjoy yourself enjoying yourself, you try to take advantage of all the 'nows' that come your way."

"Philosophy aside," Florence said, "do you realize it's nearly four years now since you've had your problems with booze and pills?"

"Who's counting," I said.

# 29
# Popsicle Molecules
# on the Tongue

For me, 1981 was an interesting mixture of "was's," "now's" and "going-to-be's."

I began the year with a determination to fulfill an ambition that Max Liebman and I had been nurturing for a long time. Tucked away in a Los Angeles warehouse, there is a treasure trove of eight years of old "Your Show of Shows" and "Caesar's Hour" kinescopes—nearly four hundred hours in all. A kinescope is a film of a live show made directly from the television screen, but, as we proved with several sample cassettes, it is readily transferable to tape. In today's hungry market for product to fill the huge number of hours on both free TV and cable, those kinescopes in the warehouse represent a bonanza of quality entertainment. Some of the material is dated, but most of the production numbers and sketches are as pertinent today as they were when we did them. We figured we could subdivide at least two hundred fifty of the kinescopes—which we jointly owned—into five hundred half-hour tapes, with newly produced introductions by me, Mel Brooks, Carl Reiner, and many of the other fine talents who worked on the shows.

We were deep into negotiations with several potential syndication buyers when Max died suddenly in July 1981. I continued the negotiations alone, representing both myself and Max's estate. At this point, the only factor holding up a deal that would enable the public to see these shows again on a regular basis is an accommodation with the Screen Actors Guild and other unions to reimburse their members who worked on the original programs. Once that is accomplished, one of my "was's" will become a "now."

I indulged myself in another "was" in the summer of 1981. Imogene Coca and I were signed to work together again in a touring stage production of a revue called *A Touch of Burlesque*. It was marvelous being back with Imogene, but I was very unhappy with the show. It was a collection of rewritten "Your Show of Shows" material and old burlesque routines, a mishmash that was neither true burlesque nor true Caesar-Coca. We were not permitted to use our creativity to inject our own peculiar flavor into the sketches.

I didn't like the show very much, but maybe I'm wrong. It drew the audiences, and then Home Box Office made a deal to tape our complete performance onstage. In 1982 *A Touch of Burlesque* began running on cable-TV systems all over the country. So who knows?

But one thing I *did* learn from *A Touch of Burlesque* was that I should never again allow myself to be locked into a situation in which I could not *contribute* creatively. I discussed this decision at great length with myself on my cassette recorder.

Well, Sidney, you went out on the road with this show and you had a great time. People came up to you, asking for your autograph, and telling you how they used to stay up late, even when they were kids, to watch you on "Your Show of Shows." But tell me the truth, shmuck, did you enjoy it? No. You've come too far. You've become too important to *yourself* to get carried away by that kind of bullshit anymore. You got those creative juices flowing again after a long, long time. So for God's sake, Sidney, use them. Don't let them freeze up again. Don't take a job just for the sake of keeping busy. If someone comes to you with a part and says not a word can be changed, tell them to shove it up their ass. There isn't a part in the world that you can't make a little better with your good brain and your good creativity, which you worked so hard to get back. So the next time, and all the other times that will come, make sure in advance that you can contribute, not just go up there and say someone else's words. Remember that, Sidney. Never forget your own self-worth.

It didn't take long before "the next time" came around. I got a call from Paramount Pictures telling me that Allan Carr, the producer, was doing a new film, *Grease II*, and that he wanted me to reprise the role of the high school football coach I had played in his original *Grease* movie in 1977. I said, "Oy." In the first place, my part in the first *Grease* hadn't been much. The incredibly successful film had been all John

Travolta and Olivia Newton-John, deservedly so. In the second place, that had been in 1977, the beginning of the darkest of my Dark Period. With the booze and the pills, I barely had known what I was doing. I just went in and read the lines they handed me. I barely knew that old friends like Eve Arden were in the cast with me.

When I got the call about *Grease II*, I said, "OK, send me a copy of the script. After I read it, I'll let you know."

The script arrived, and the football coach's part was just as *blech* as it had been before. I was about to turn it down, but I began to think. It was just like the old days, when I got my ideas from nearly every little thing I saw on the street, or in the subway, or in movies and plays. I remembered all the insipid interviews with coaches between the halves of football and basketball games, in which they kept using the clichés about how life is just like the game their kids are playing, and how the kids are being prepared for Life, with a capital *L*, by slam-dunking a basketball or kicking a field goal.

I picked up the phone and called my agent, Tom Korman. I said to Tom, "Who's the director on this picture?"

He said, "Pat Birch. You remember her. She's that very bright young woman who was the choreographer on the original *Grease*."

I said, "Set up an appointment for me to talk to her, will you?"

The picture was shooting at the unused Excelsior High School building in Norwalk, about an hour outside of Los Angeles, so I had to drive down there to see her. I was determined to lay it on the line: if I couldn't change my part to incorporate my own ideas, I wouldn't do it.

When I arrived, Pat was busy rehearsing a scene, so I

wandered around the cafeteria and said hello to Eve Arden, Dody Goodman, Tom Poston, Tab Hunter, and some other members of the cast whom I knew.

Suddenly someone was tugging at my elbow. It was Pat. She's a little woman, hardly as big as the actors playing the high school kids, and I had trouble seeing who it was at first. She greeted me warmly and we grabbed trays of cafeteria food and went to her office to talk. She was using the office of the vice-principal of the school.

The story of what happened after that would be better coming from her.

## Pat Birch

*When I found Sid wandering around in the cafeteria, I was amazed at how he had changed. The changes became ever more apparent to me when I got him into the quiet of my office. In the first picture, he had been thin and sickly looking and hardly ever said very much. This had shocked me because I had grown up as a teenager idolizing this big, powerful comic genius for whom I would turn down dates if they wouldn't stay home with me on Saturday nights to watch "Your Show of Shows" and "Caesar's Hour."*

*Now, looking at Sid and listening to him in my office, I was delighted to realize that the Caesar of old was back. At that time, I had no idea of the terrible sickness he had been through or that he had cured himself with the same Jungian techniques I had heard about from my great dance teacher, Martha Graham.*

*When we got down to the business at hand, Sid said to me that he would only take the coach's role if I would let him put*

271

*some of his own ideas into it. I said, "Christ, yes. What* are *some of your ideas?"*

*He said, "Well, coaches are always talking in these clichés and that's how I want my guy to be. I'll give you a for-instance. He tells his players, 'Everything in life is like a football game. Take war. In war, the other team throws a nuclear bomb at you, see. So what do you have to do? You have to intercept that bomb downfield, deep in your own territory, and then you toss that bomb right back into the other guy's end zone.' "*

*I said, "That's* marvelous. *We'll use it. Tell me more." Sid gave me some other examples of how this idiot coach would talk. Then Ken Finkleman came in. Ken is the writer of the* Grease II *script and a big Caesar fan from when he was not more than ten years old. Ken was delighted with the changes Sid had proposed and we were in business.*

*But that wasn't all. Before Sid left that day, I said to him, "This is the first time I've ever directed comedy scenes, and who knows more about comedy than you? Would you help me out as sort of an unofficial consultant, even in the scenes where you're not working?" He said, "Sure," and that's what he did for several weeks.*

*His own scenes were gems, but he was even more important to me in the* shtick *involving the high school kids alone. He'd sit quietly to one side of the set, and I'd keep looking at him. If the kids were doing a funny scene correctly, he'd nod. If something was wrong, he'd shake his head. It was then that I'd stop and ask his advice. In one key scene, for example, Tab Hunter, a teacher, is giving his class its first sex education lecture. The scene was written for the kids to indulge in a lot of horseplay while Tab talks about how you conceive, and things like that. It just wasn't working, not funny at all.*

*I went over to Sid and asked, "What do I do?" He said,*

*"Play it for embarrassment, not the kidding around. I did a skit like that once. Kids get very embarrassed when sex is openly discussed in class for the first time. Do it with the kids giggling nervously, and not able to look each other in the eye, and turd-kicking—and you'll get a lot of laughs." I tried it that way, and he was right.*

*All in all, I can say that Sid not only juiced up his own part but he helped change the tone of the entire picture. It's crazier and much zanier than it would have been if he hadn't been there.*

It's very kind of Pat to say such nice things about me. I can't say enough about *her*. My role in *Grease II* is not a major one, and the picture is hardly a milestone in my overall career. But this lovely, understanding woman helped me enormously in my continuing effort to "be important to myself."

That is a never-ending process for me, and sometimes the instigations that propel it come from the least-expected sources. Late in 1981, for example, I got a phone call out of the blue from the Dancer Fitzgerald Sample advertising agency in New York. They were launching a new TV and radio campaign for Popsicles, and they wanted to use my know-it-all Professor character from "Your Show of Shows" and "Caesar's Hour."

I said, as I had to Pat Birch, "Only if I can contribute."

The agency people were puzzled. They said, "But we have our own writers, Mr. Caesar, and commercials are a very specialized art form. How do you mean 'contribute'?"

Lapsing into the Professor's German accent, I ad-libbed: "I'll gif you a example—from physics, which I know all about. The molecules from the cherries, they are all in the vat where you make Popsicles, and they're so happy they're all dancing around and holding hands, and they suddenly, poof! they get frozen in time. That's so they can't fall off the stick. *Then* when the heat of the tongue releases the cherry molecules from the prison of the frozen time, they're so happy that the hugging and the kissing and the joy that goes on your tongue, it's unbelievable."

The Dancer Fitzgerald people said, "We'll be right out to see you, Mr. Caesar."

A whole delegation of them showed up at my house in California. We immediately got to work. Following the lead of my ad-lib on the telephone, the agency's writers had come up with some good ideas, and I came up with some more ideas—all based on the Professor's crazy notions of physics and how they apply to the deliciousness of the Popsicle products. Specialized art form or not, it was no different from the tossing around of concepts in the writers' room of "Your Show of Shows," and I was delighted, as I always am, to be part of such a creative melee again.

One of our best ideas involves a Popsicle product called the Sidewalk Sundae. The Professor, in discussing the dark-brown fudge center of the Sidewalk Sundae, compares it with a Black Hole somewhere out in the universe: "The Black Hole is so powerful not even light can get out, so if not even light can escape, how is the flavor going to get out of there? So if the flavor it's not going anyvhere, it's all going to be vaiting for you right there in the Black Hole." Or something like that.

In any event, in case you've been wondering, that's how I got to be the radio and TV spokesman for the Popsicle Company.

It was all a part of the molecules of my own personal creativity becoming active once again, after my emergence from my own personal Black Hole.

As I said, it's a continuing process—part of my continuing recovery.

In my career, I have become severely analytical in evaluating the scripts that are constantly sent to me by producers and studios who have me in mind to play a certain role in their movies and TV projects. I'm flattered and I read them all. There was a time when I'd turn the scripts over to an agent or an assistant and rely on their synopses and their judgments as to whether I should consider taking the part or not.

No more. Now I alone consider each proposal, and my decision is based on one key factor. I have enough sense of my self-worth now so that I will only do what I think is right for *me*.

I also spend a lot of time developing my *own* properties, with the help of various talented writers. I've already mentioned my projected movie, which will be a comic spoof of all science fiction movies. There are many, many more—including some in which I will get away from comedy completely and do serious drama, including playing villainous heavies. I have finally come to believe everyone who has told me that I'm an actor, not just a *comic* actor.

Creativity. Constantly keeping my mind busy. Substituting positive addictions for negative addictions.

That's the name of the game for me.

# 30
# Hands on the Carriage

With all the creativity bubbling around in my head, I still had to work. That, too, is part of my therapy. As Jack Benny once said, "I act because that is what I do." For me, it always was easy to pick up a dinner-theater engagement to fill in my time. And since *Last of the Red Hot Lovers* is fun for me to do because I can fool around with it and use my creativity to change it each time, I kept performing it in dinner-theaters whenever I was asked.

And that's how I happened to be in Clarksville, Indiana, just across the Ohio River from Louisville, Kentucky, in January 1982. I didn't know this was going to be a test of the New Me. Or maybe I *did* realize it, subliminally. Why else would I elect to do *Last of the Red Hot Lovers* for five weeks in the midst of the worst weather the Midwest had seen in the last hundred years?

The show itself went fine. I had a good director and an excellent supporting cast. By some miracle, a sizable audience managed to find its way nearly every night to the Derby Playhouse, where we were doing the play. Neither rain nor sleet nor blizzard nor below-zero cold managed to stay them from coming to eat prime rib and watching us work.

The potential problems arose in the many hours of the day when I was *not* working. I was totally alone. The weather being what it was, I didn't want to subject Florence to it. I had no one to talk to except my cassette recorder. It was a lot like Paris—except that this wasn't Paris. I could scarcely go out without risking frostbite.

It was a situation in which I would have gone completely to pieces in the old days. My hotel was a modern one, a Hilton, but no hotel is equipped to handle wind-chill factors of forty-five degrees below zero. Especially with today's glass-wall construction. So I sat in my room, dressed in my overcoat, hat, and gloves. I read a lot, but it was difficult to turn the pages of a book wearing mittens. The hotel management sent up a space heater to supplement the regular heating system. I was alternately too hot and too cold.

I did my exercises and I made a deal with the chef—a very nice man—to prepare my special diet for me. He made my "mush" just right. Sometimes, however, it would be half-frozen, like a parfait, before I could get around to eating it.

On the few sunny, fairly warm days, I would take walks. About a half mile down the river, I made a fascinating discovery. There was a huge dam there, across the Ohio River. I'd study it for hours at a time—for as long as I could stand the cold—because it reminded me of my interpretation of Einstein's theory of Relativity.

There was all this water going *over* the dam and accomplishing absolutely nothing. To me, this wasted water represented all the "nows" I had let slip by in my life. These "nows," like the wasted water, never became "was's." On the other hand, there was a different volume of water going through the dam's sluices. These were "nows" that were being taken advantage of. The water was churning around in the sluices, turning turbines, and producing an enormous amount of energy. These were "nows" becoming "was's" and eventually "going-to-be's," in terms of what could be done with the electricity they produced.

It was all fanciful and conceptual, but it very successfully kept my mind where it belonged—on the positive rather than the negative.

The negative aspects of this trip were not yet over. When the show's run ended after five weeks and it was time for me to go home, a travel agent booked me on what was supposed to be a nonstop flight from Louisville to Los Angeles.

I got on the plane, and only then did I learn that because of the weather and poststrike air controller situation, the flight would make stops in Atlanta, Baton Rouge, Dallas, and God knows where else along the way. A four-hour trip was going to take seven hours or longer.

The Old Me would have torn up airports, screamed and yelled at airline personnel, and become generally obnoxious. I then would have swallowed a handful of pills and drunk all the booze the stewardesses would have handed out. The Old Me would have looked for immediate oblivion to blot out the ordeal and to punish myself for all the uproar I had caused.

The New Me didn't even vaguely consider these methods. I just said to myself, "Well, Sidney, we've got a real fuck-up here, but what can you do about it? Nothing. So what's the worst that will happen? You'll sit and you'll read and you'll get to Los Angeles a few hours later. So then you'll go home and Maranee will have a nice hot meal waiting for you, and you'll enjoy being in your house with Florence and Karen, and what will you lose except a few hours? This is a bad "now," Sidney, but make it into a good "now" and it will turn into a good "was.""

I made myself comfortable in my seat on the airplane and pulled out a copy of Barbara Tuchman's *Guns of August*. I read for a couple of hours and fell peacefully asleep. Barbara Tuchman always puts me to sleep.

I didn't get home until after midnight, and only the dogs, Conus and Sascha, greeted me. Everyone else was in bed.

I quietly soaked up the beauties of the house. Then, before I awakened Florence, I had something to do. I took my cassette recorder out of my bag and walked down the hall to the room I use as an office. On the way, I stopped to look at a painting I had done in my Dark Period, many years before. At that time, I had taken art lessons and was seeking release with oils and canvas. It is a very ugly painting, almost demonic in concept, but I always thought it had a certain style. The main focus of the picture is a human fetus in a bottle, with an atomic mushroom cloud spurting from the top of the bottle. What did it mean? How the hell did I know?

But looking at that painting again at the end of the Louisville trip, I noticed something for the first time. The bottle that contained the fetus was a *whiskey* bottle.

"Boy-oh-boy-oh-boy-oh-boy," I said to myself.

When I got to my office, I flicked on the cassette recorder

and had a conversation with Sidney about how he came through the test of the rigorous Clarksville-Louisville experience.

Well, Sidney, you ought to be proud of yourself. Do you realize what you *used* to do under circumstances like that? You've learned, Sidney. How *much* you have learned. And do you know what's the most important thing you've learned? Remember that recurring nightmare you used to have about when you were a baby and your brother Dave let your carriage roll down the hill, and you were so frightened because suddenly there were no hands on the carriage? Well, you don't have that nightmare anymore, do you, Sidney? You know why, Sidney? Because, like this terrible trip proved, you're at the controls. There *are* hands on the carriage now. Your *own* hands, Sidney, your own strong hands. Maybe symbolically they're your father's hands, because you've become your own father. But who cares? Hands are hands. As long as they're on the carriage. Keep remembering that, Sidney. Never let yourself forget it. Good-night, friend.